Introduction.

To begin, thank you for buying this book, and a huge thanks to all the artists who have contributed, the teachers who helped out, and all the people who helped get the project started.

Alex and I started this both as a practical way for artists to respond and raise money for people, and as a small way to try and get something positive going from the mess left behind by the floods. If we can continue to involve people in producing art, whether for colouring books or just for the sake of it, then it's been worth the effort.

Having been through the floods of 2009 in Cockermouth, I was particularly keen to involve schools in this, and give the children and young adults a bit of a say. Amongst all the grownup talk of insurance premiums and EU reconstruction grants and property values, the voice of the younger generation gets lost, and it was their floods too. So we've included some work from Cockermouth School, Appleby School, and the Queen Elizabeth Grammar School in Penrith.

We haven't put the pictures in any particular order, beyond putting Chris Riddell's first, because he's the Children's Laureate, so it seems a bit rude not to. The others are more or less in the order they arrived, but with the children's contributions in the second part of the book.

We hope you enjoy colouring in the book, and that one day we might see the results, online or in person,

Gavin Pollock, and Alex Jakob-Whitworth

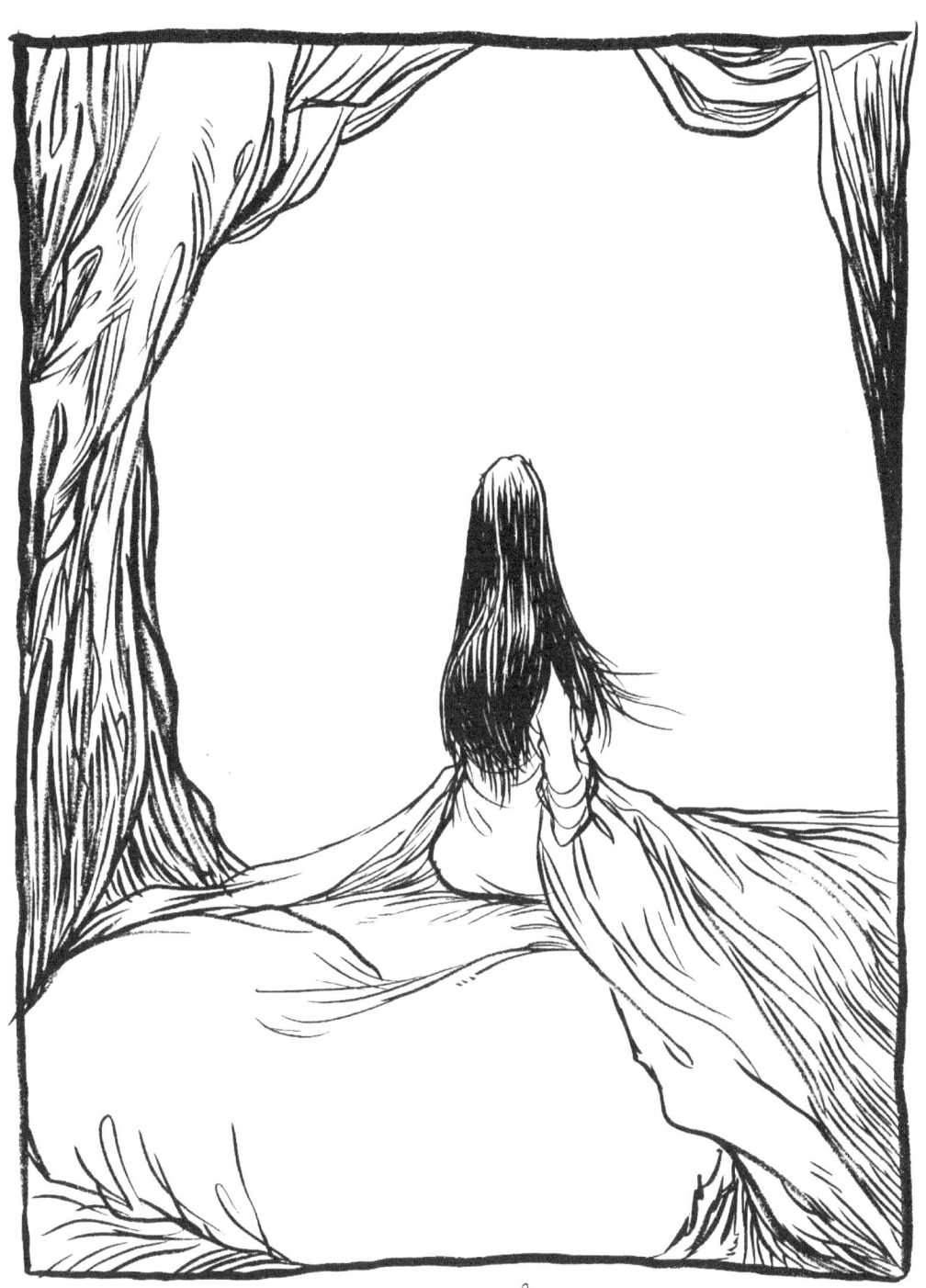

Morning

Chris Riddell

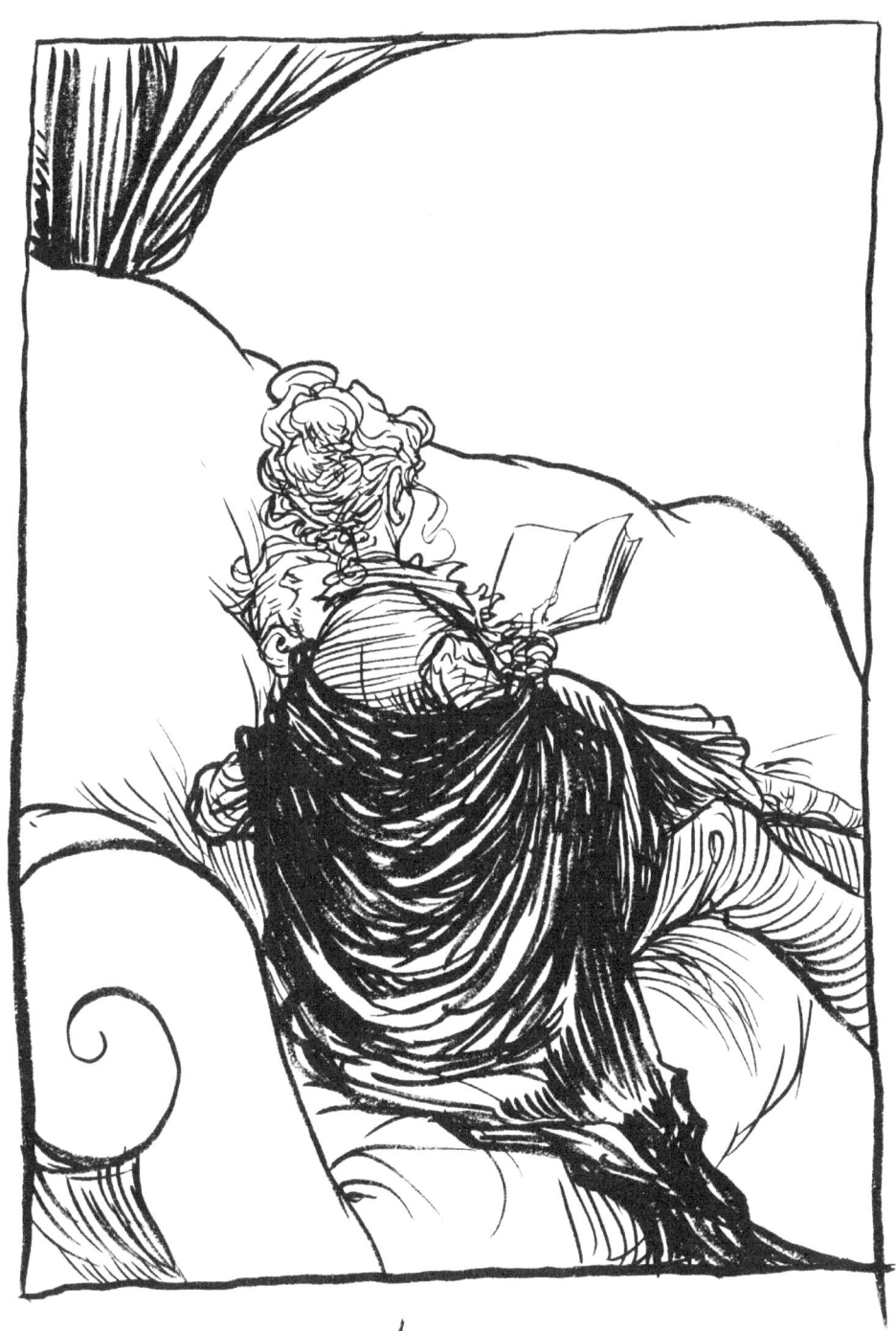

# Afternoon

Chris Riddell

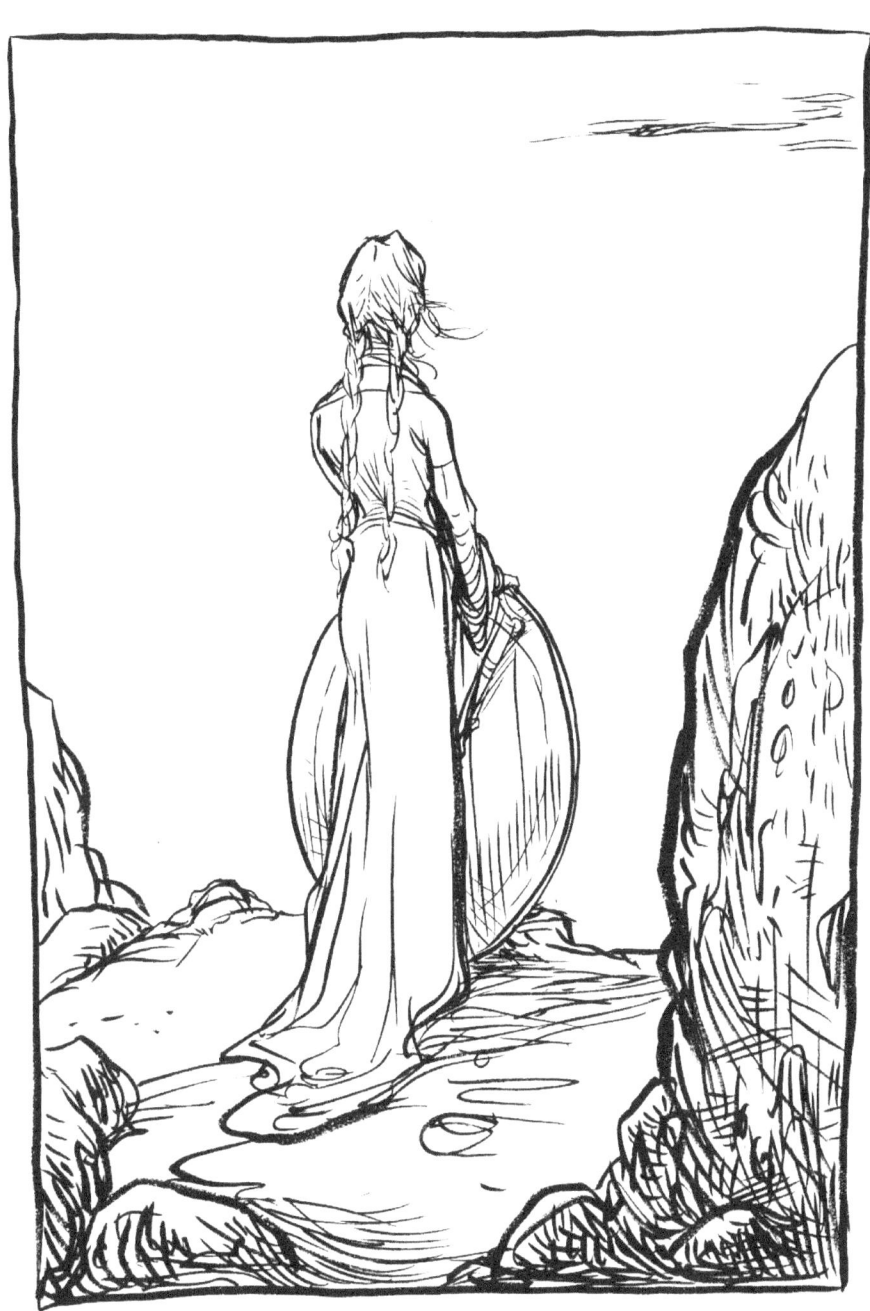

Evening

Chris Riddell

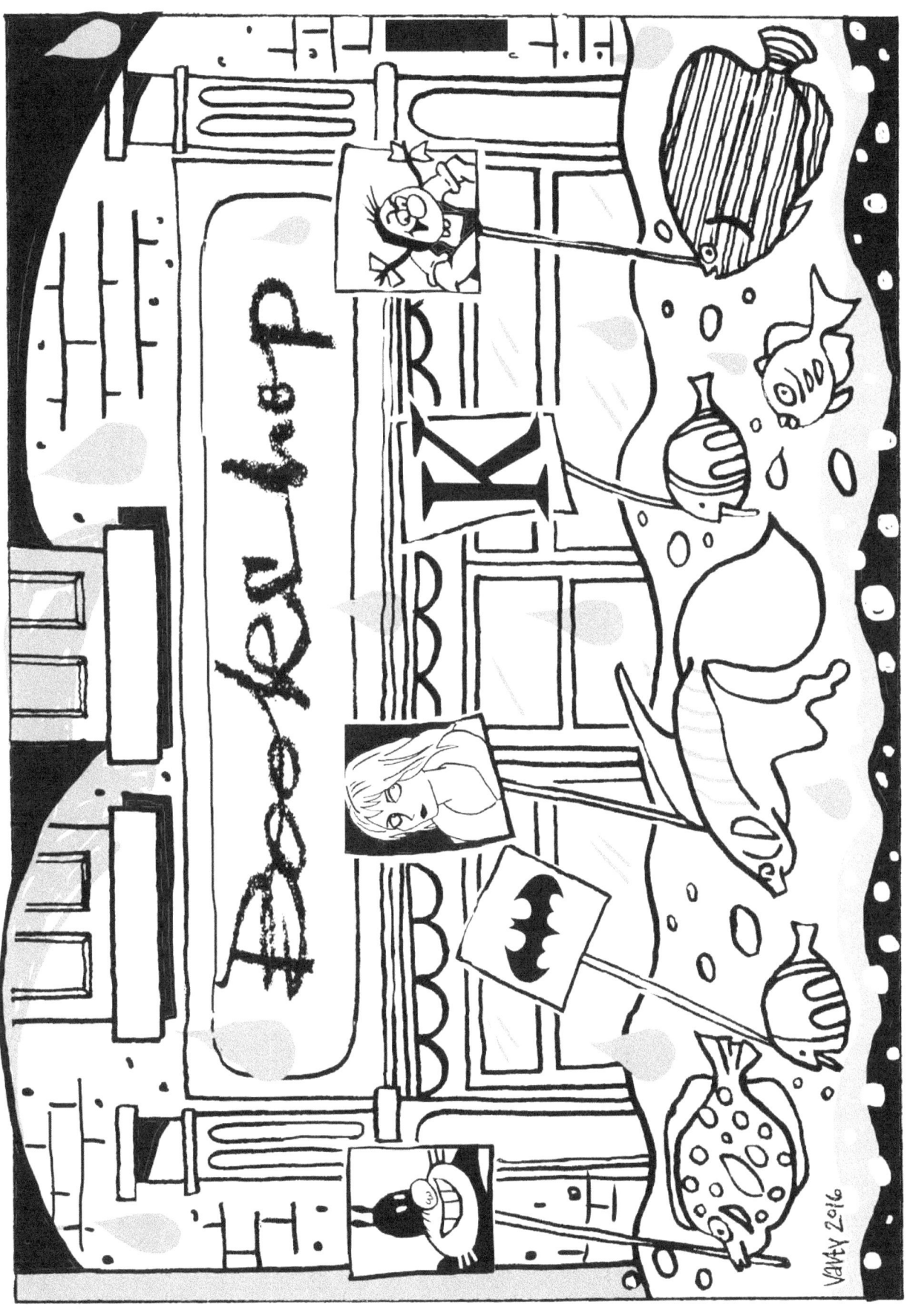

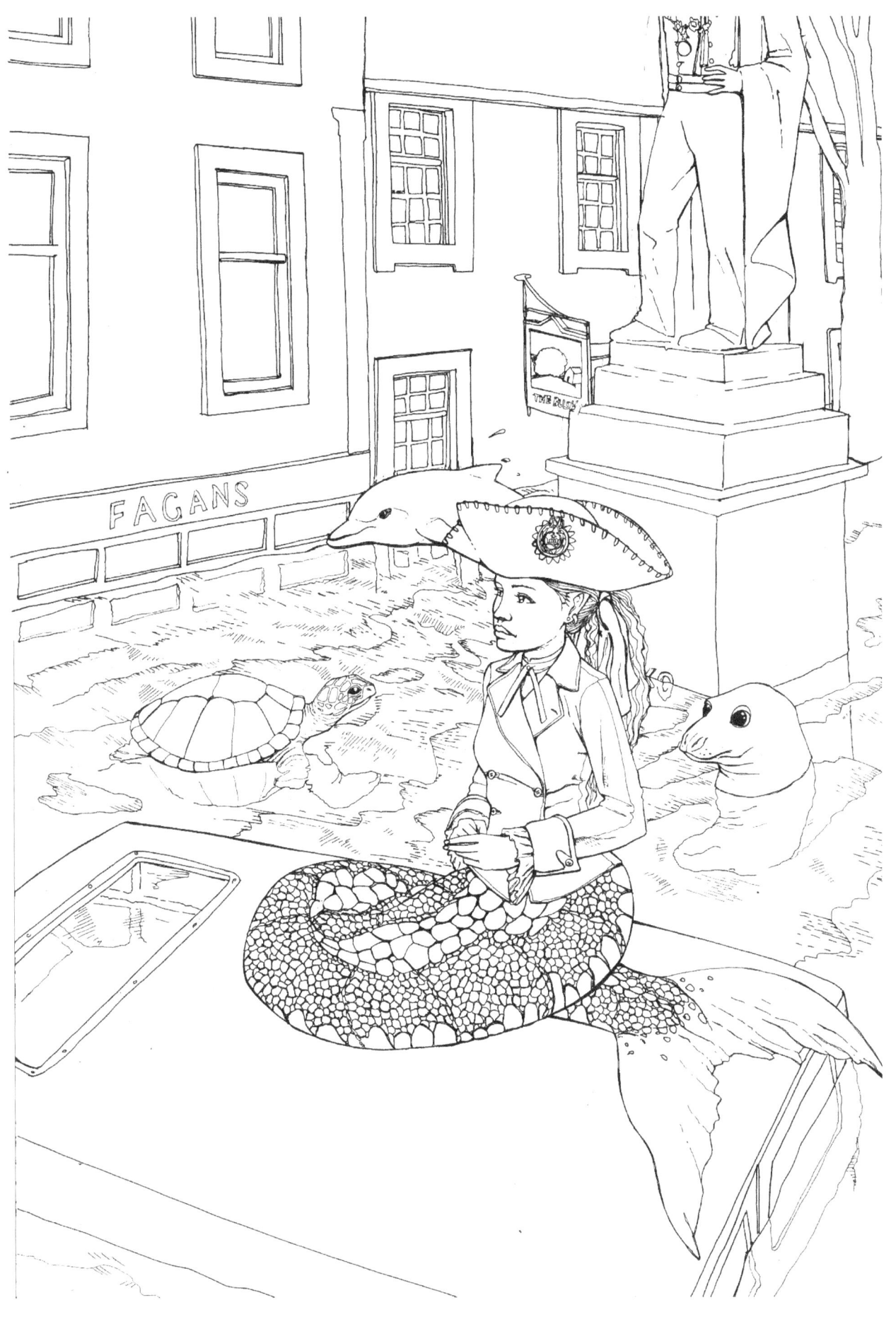

Gavin Pollock

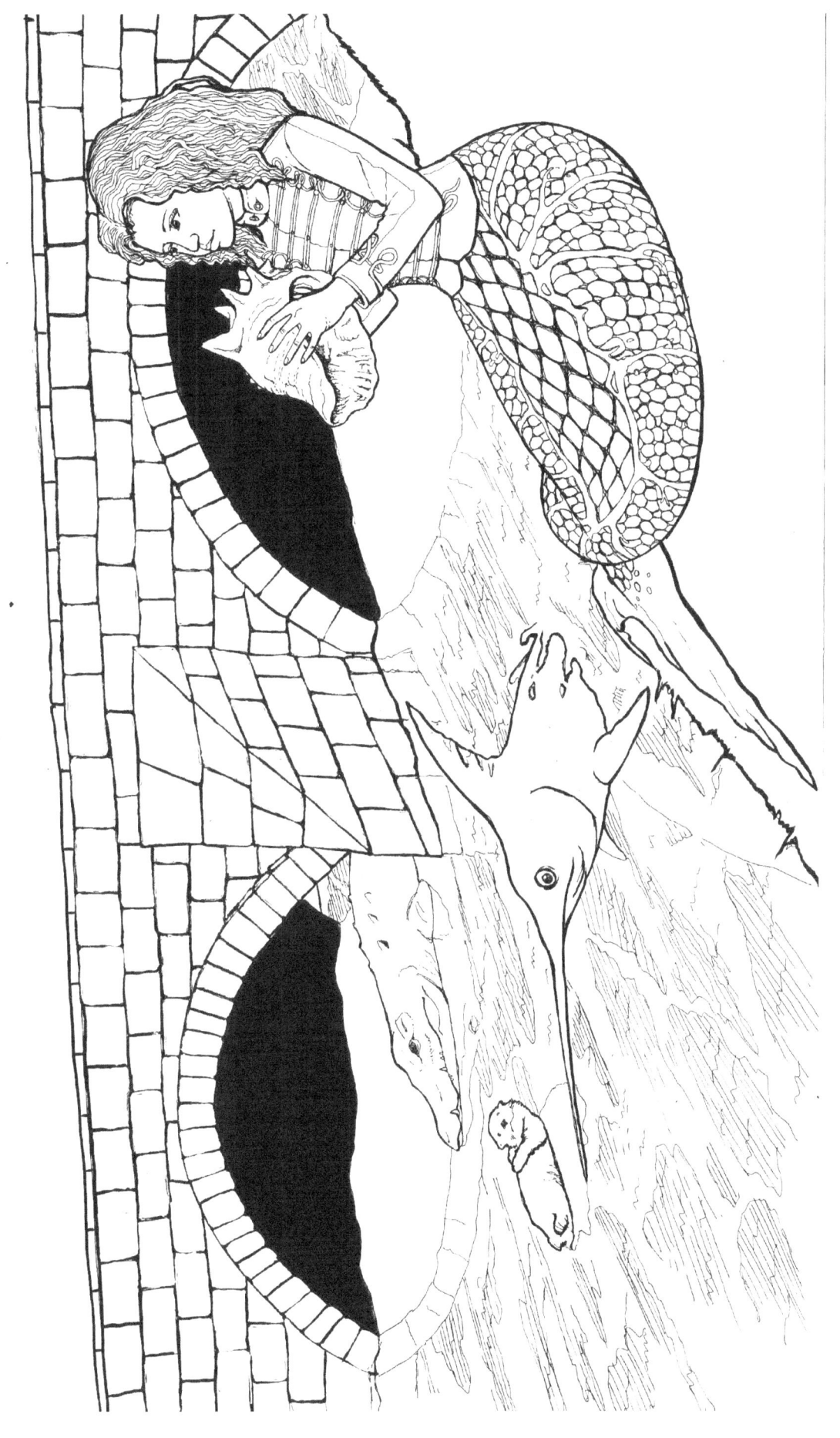

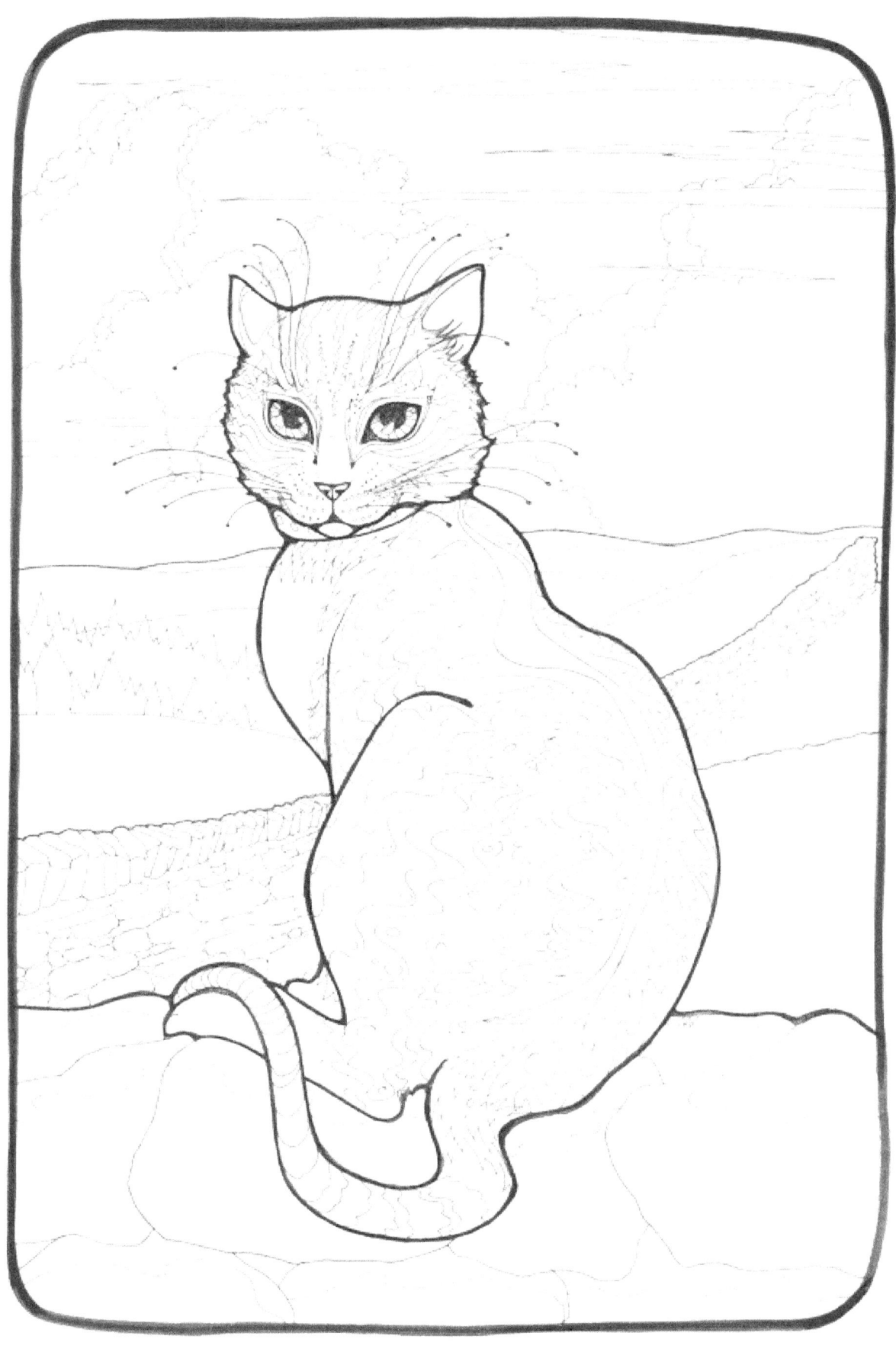

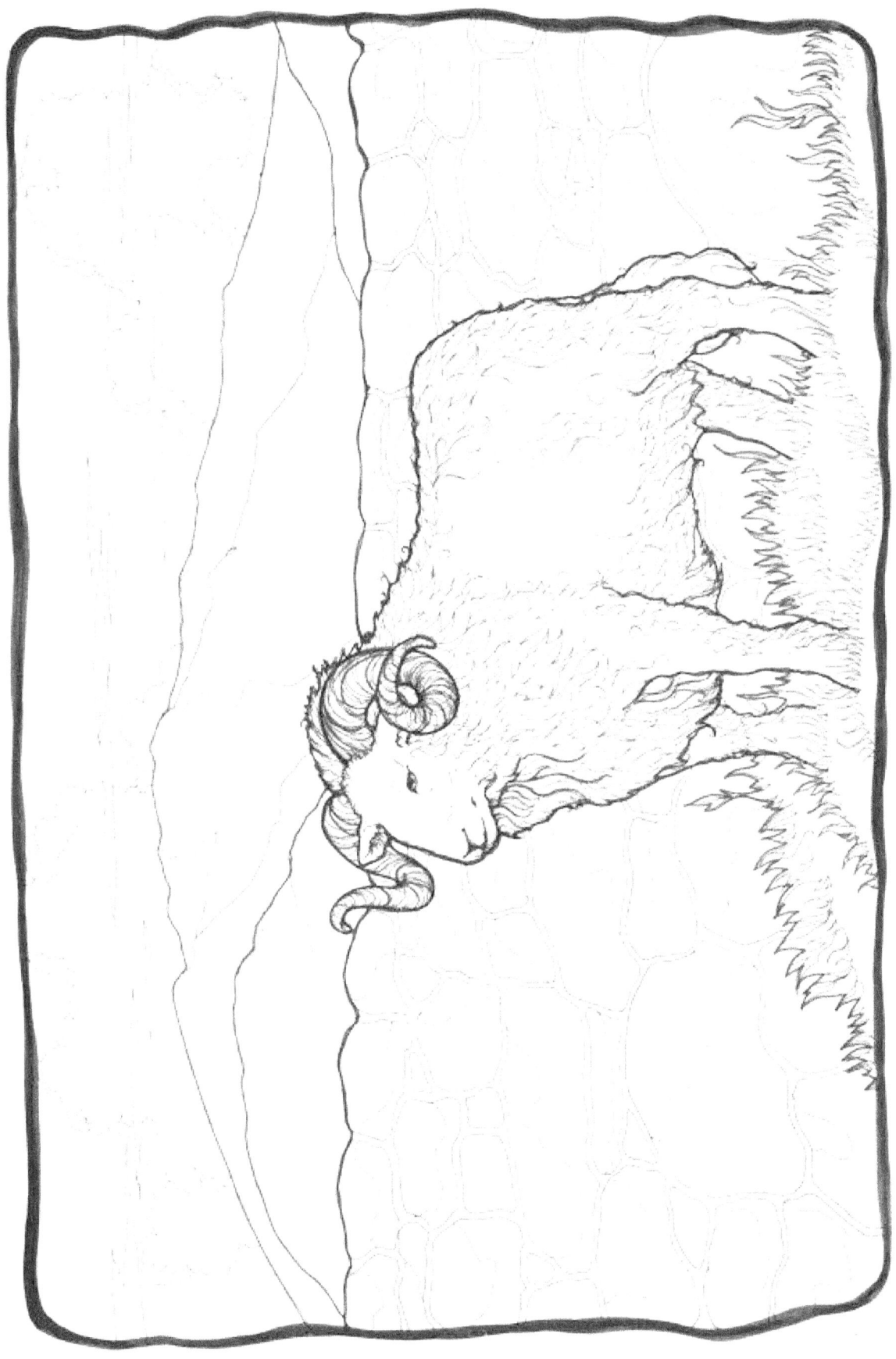

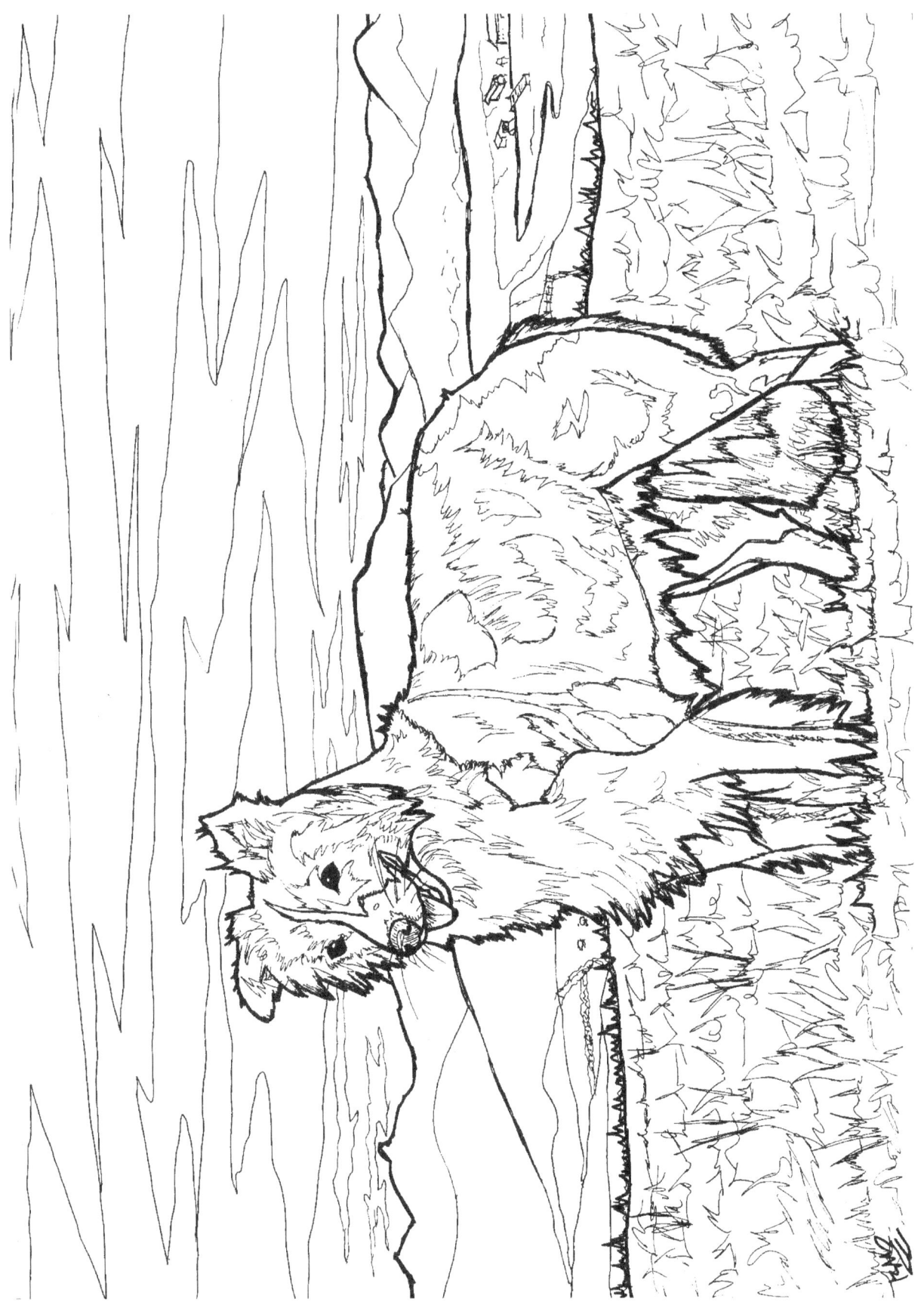

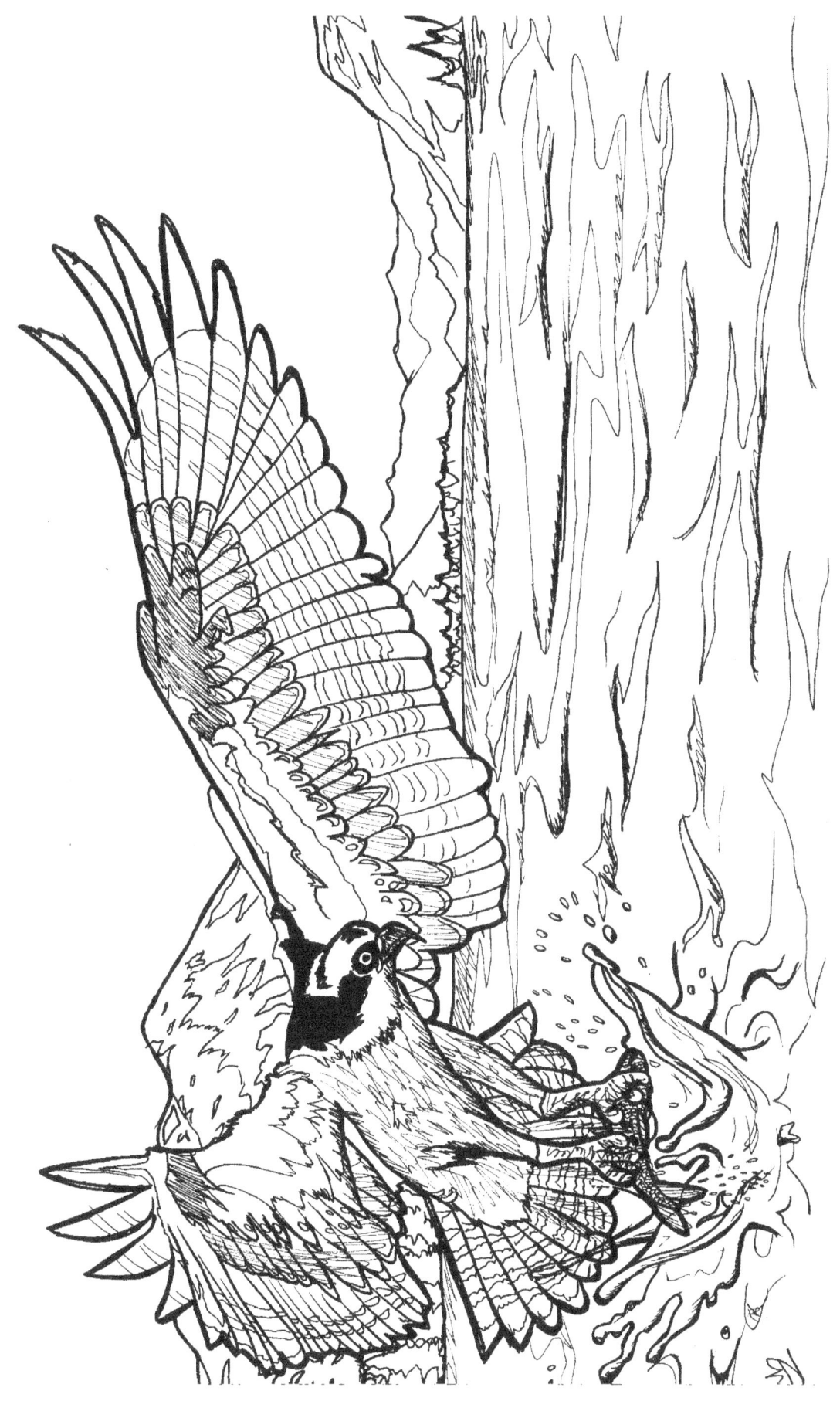

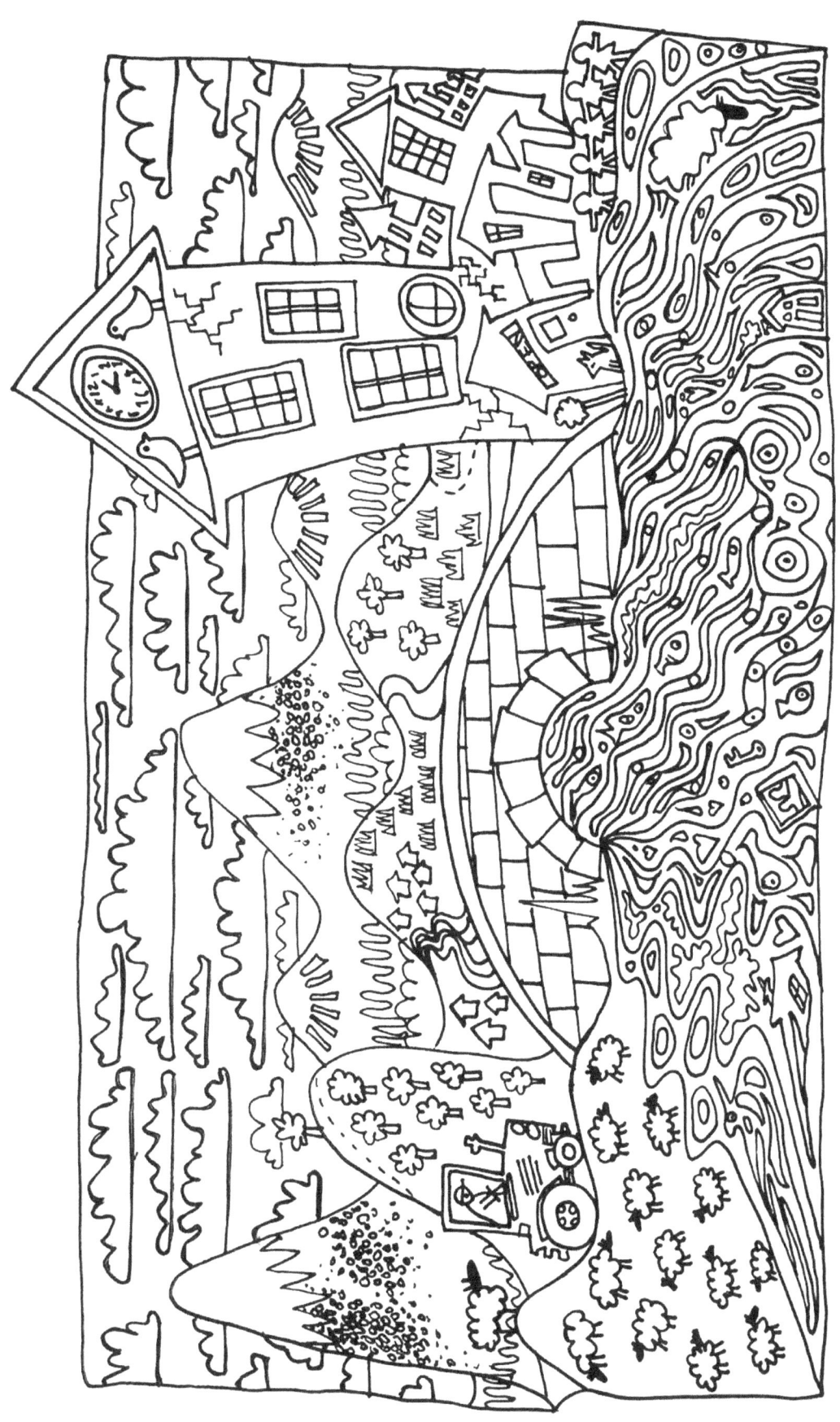

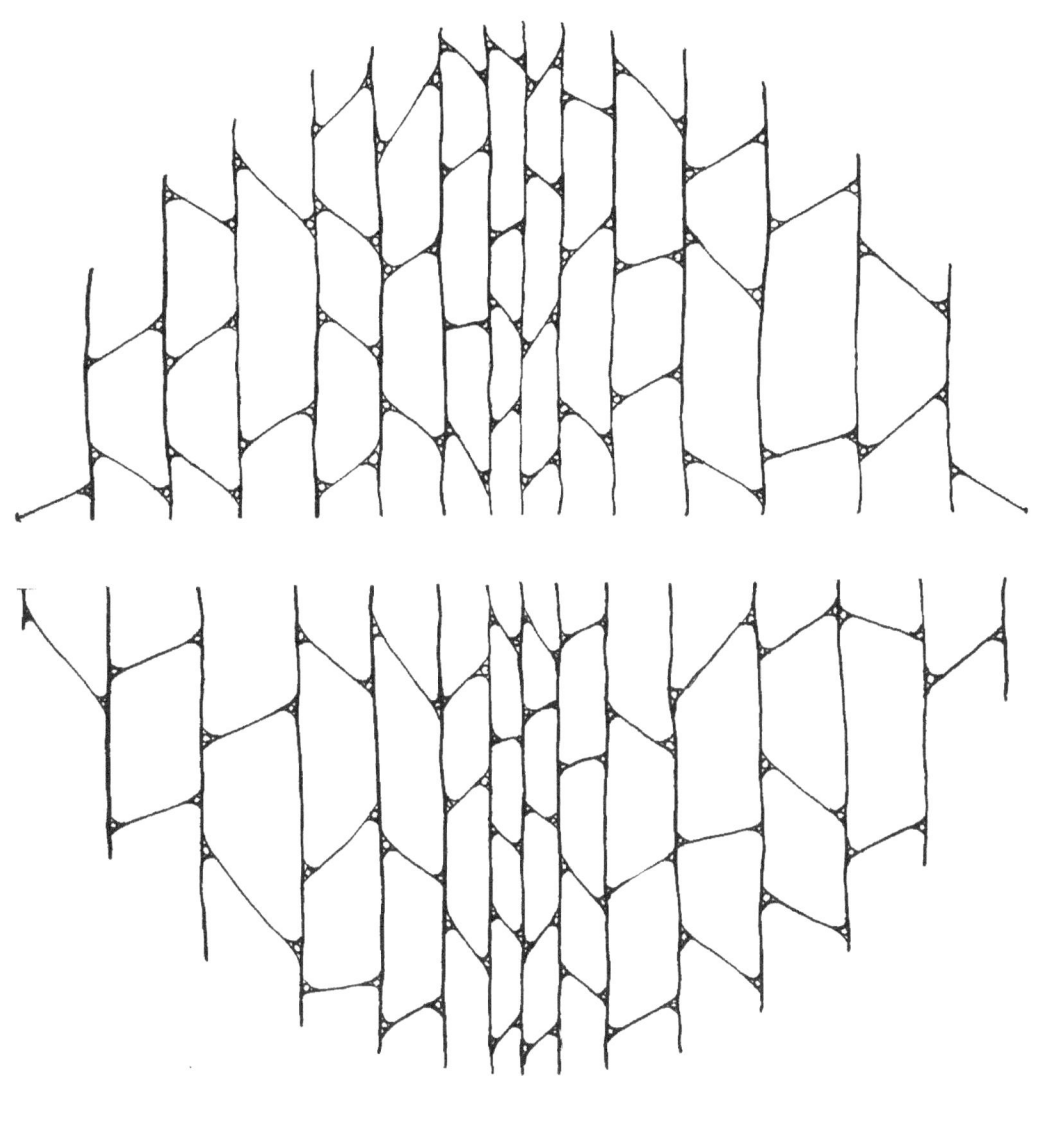

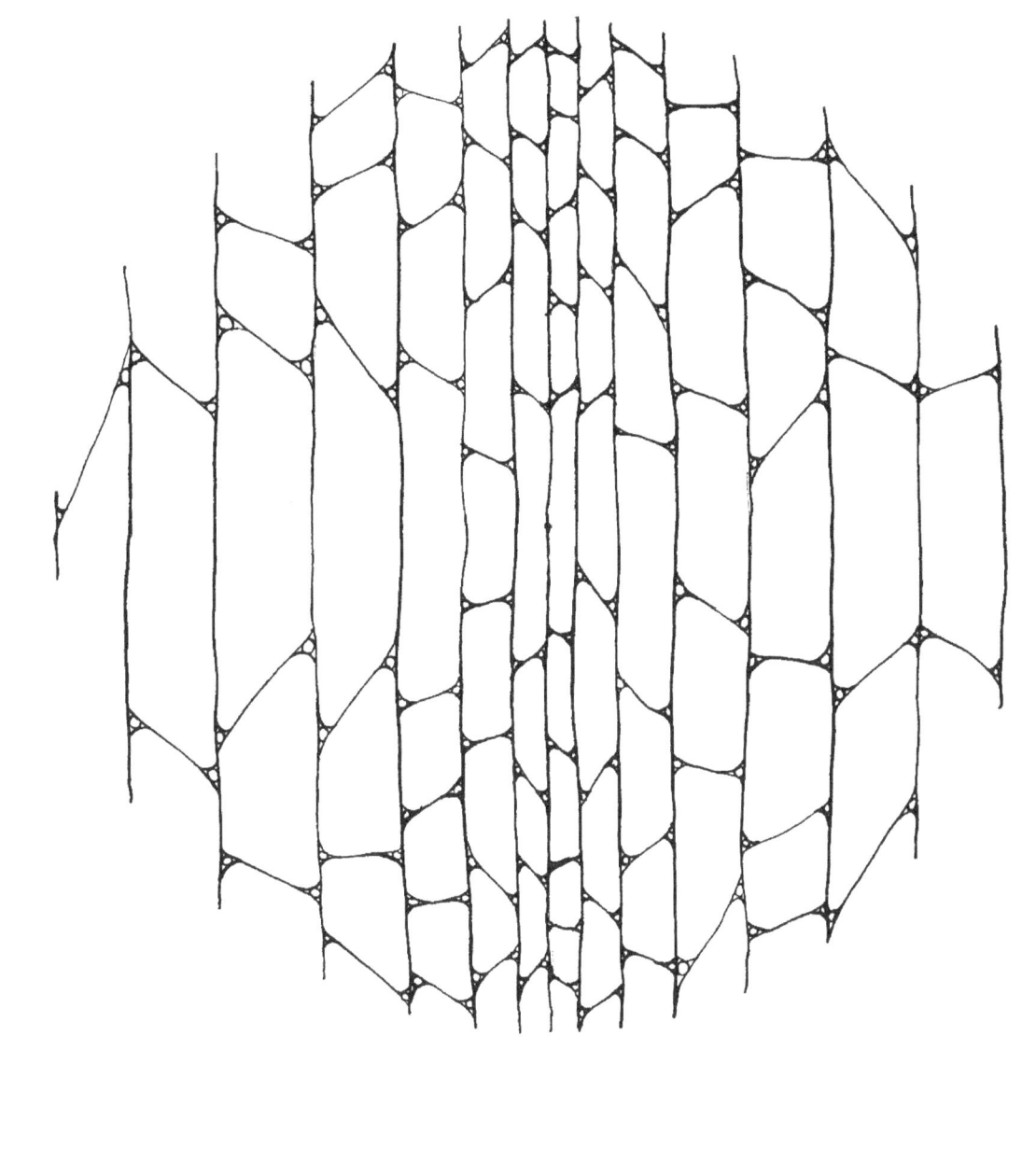

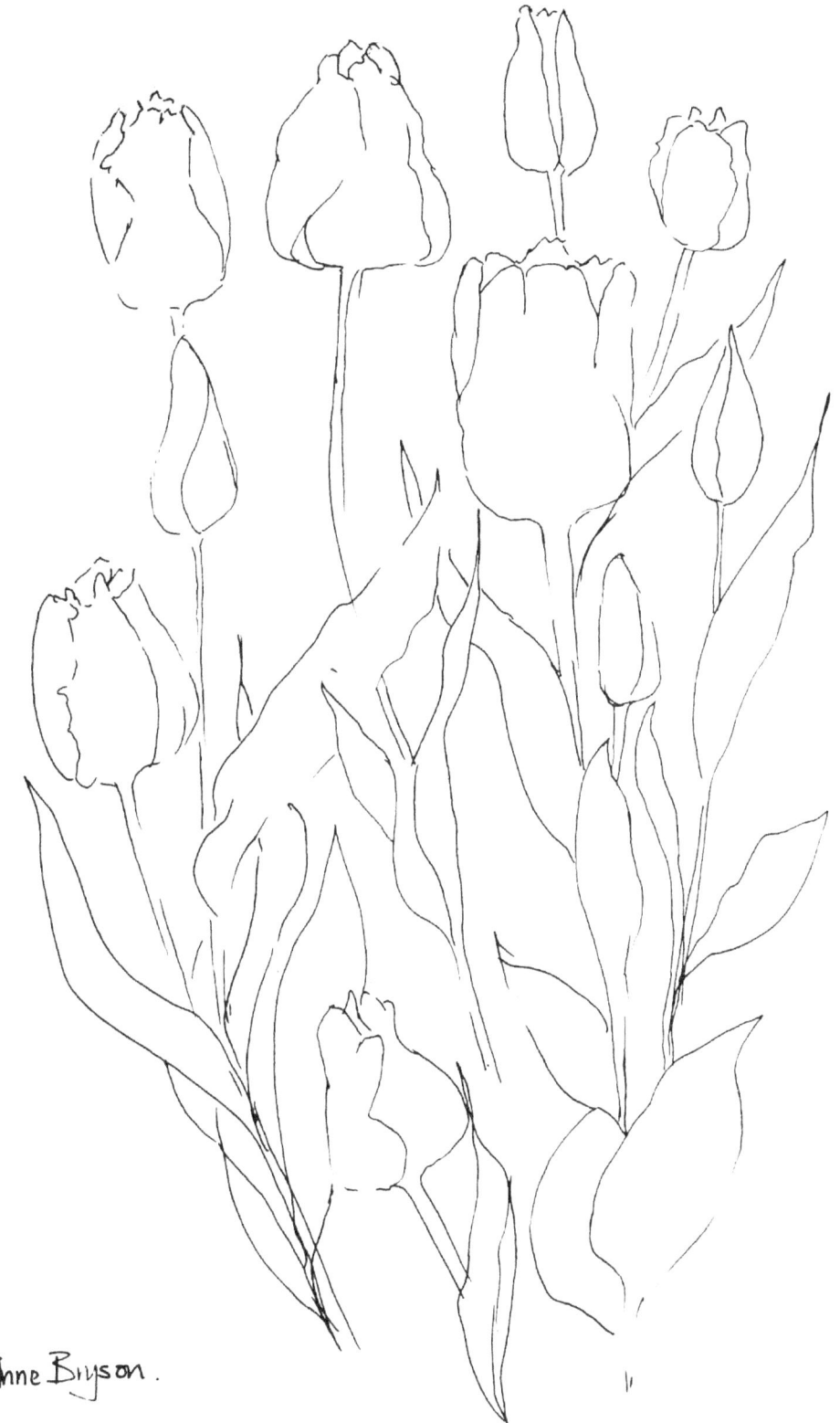

Anne Bryson.

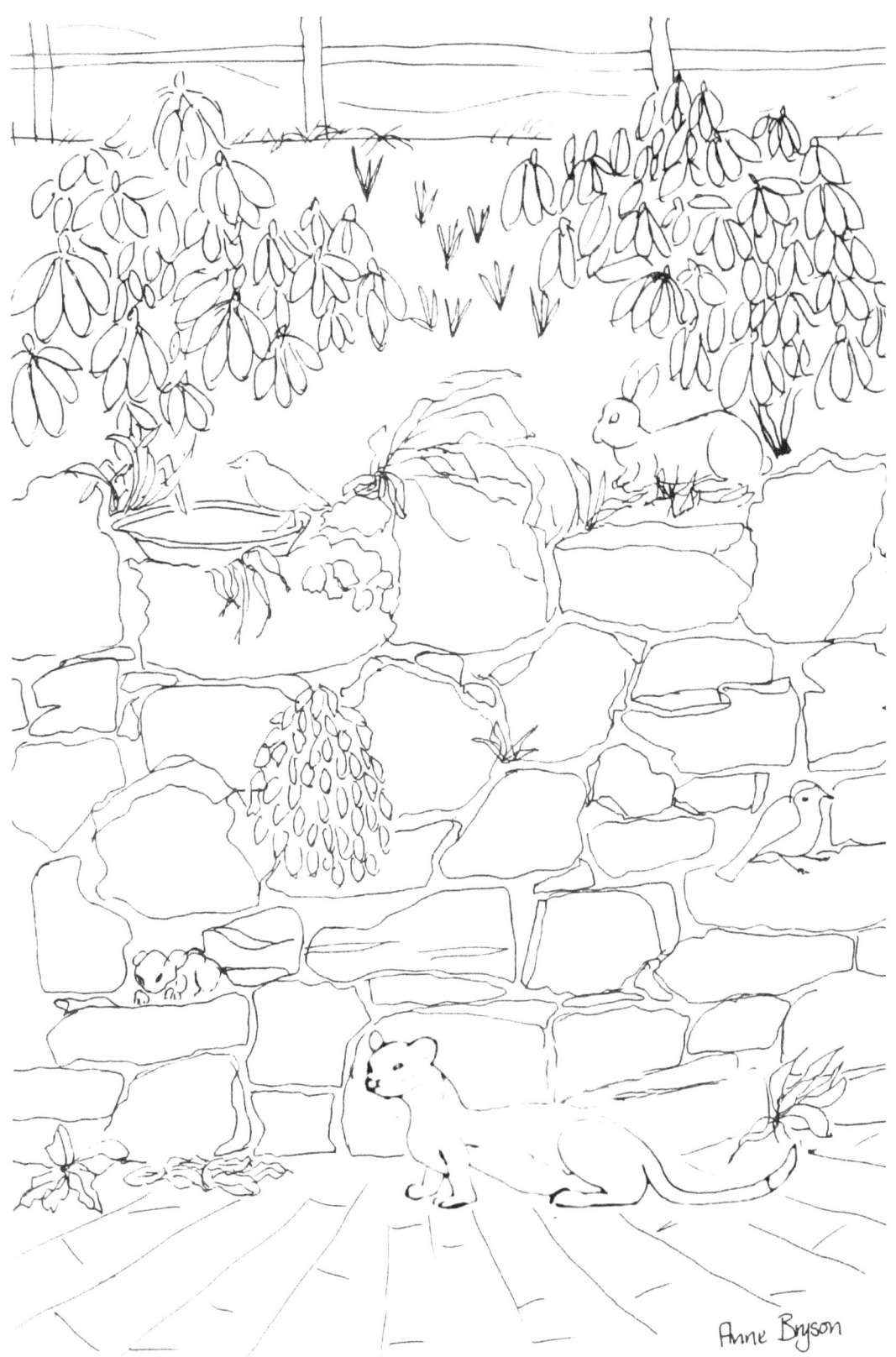

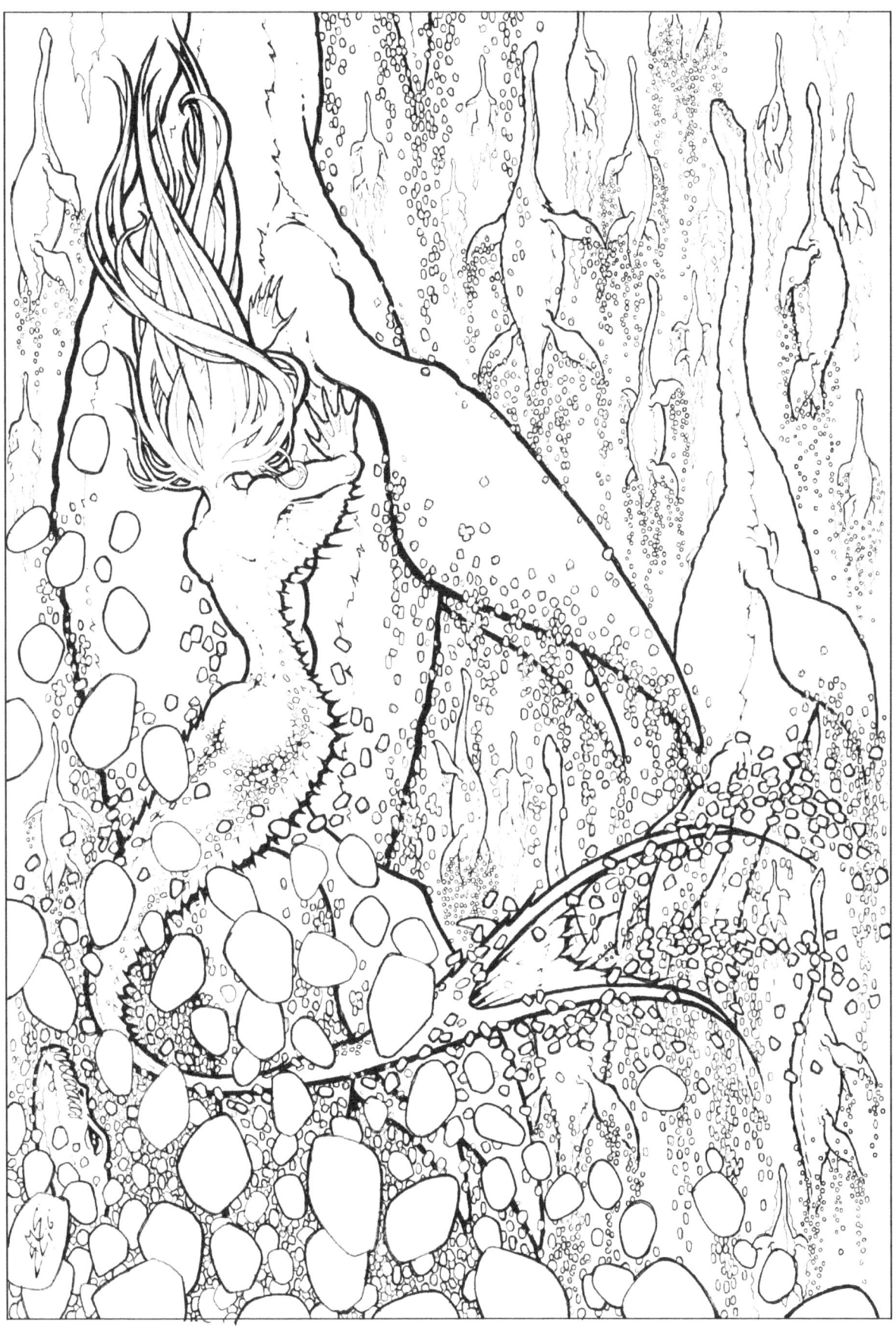

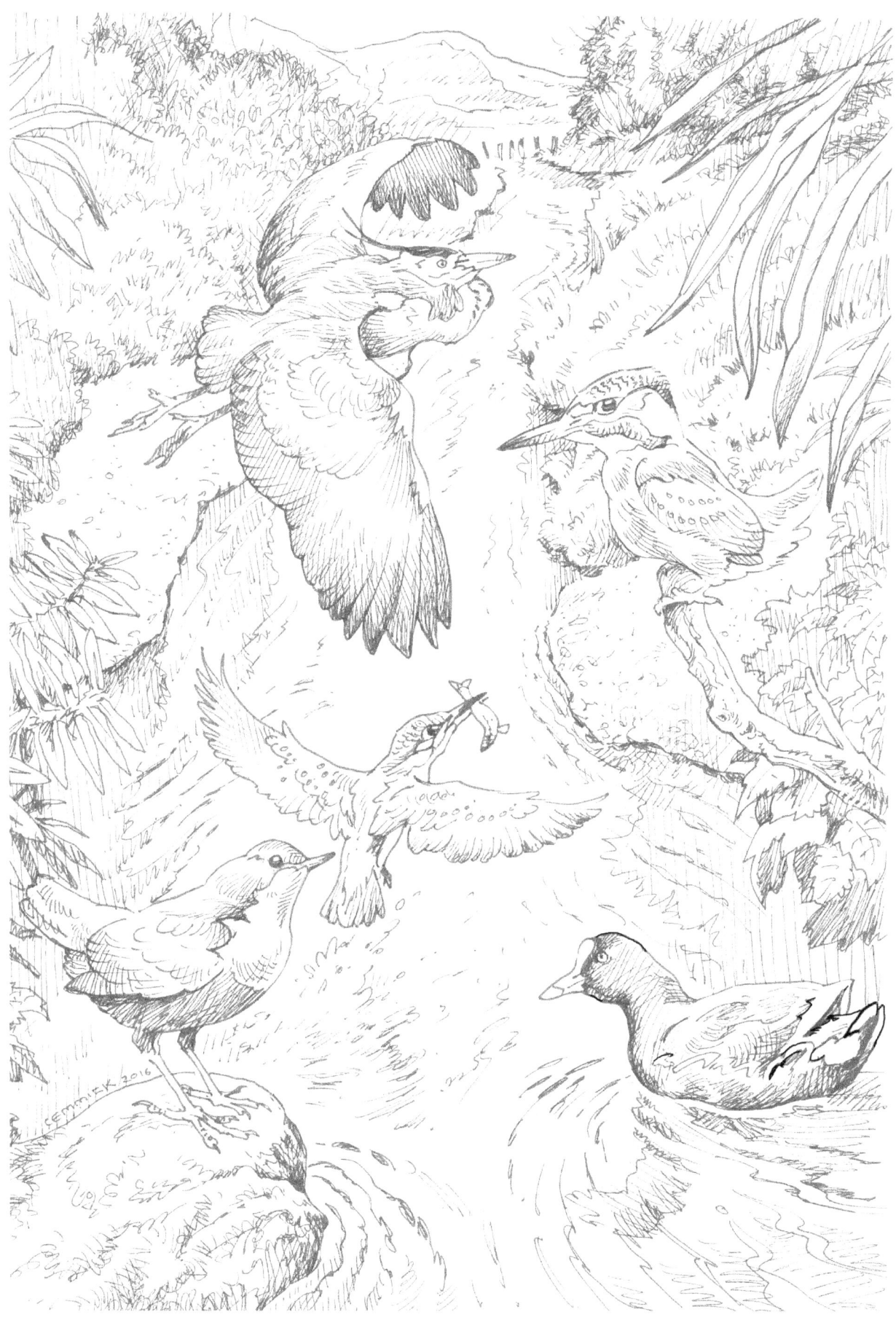

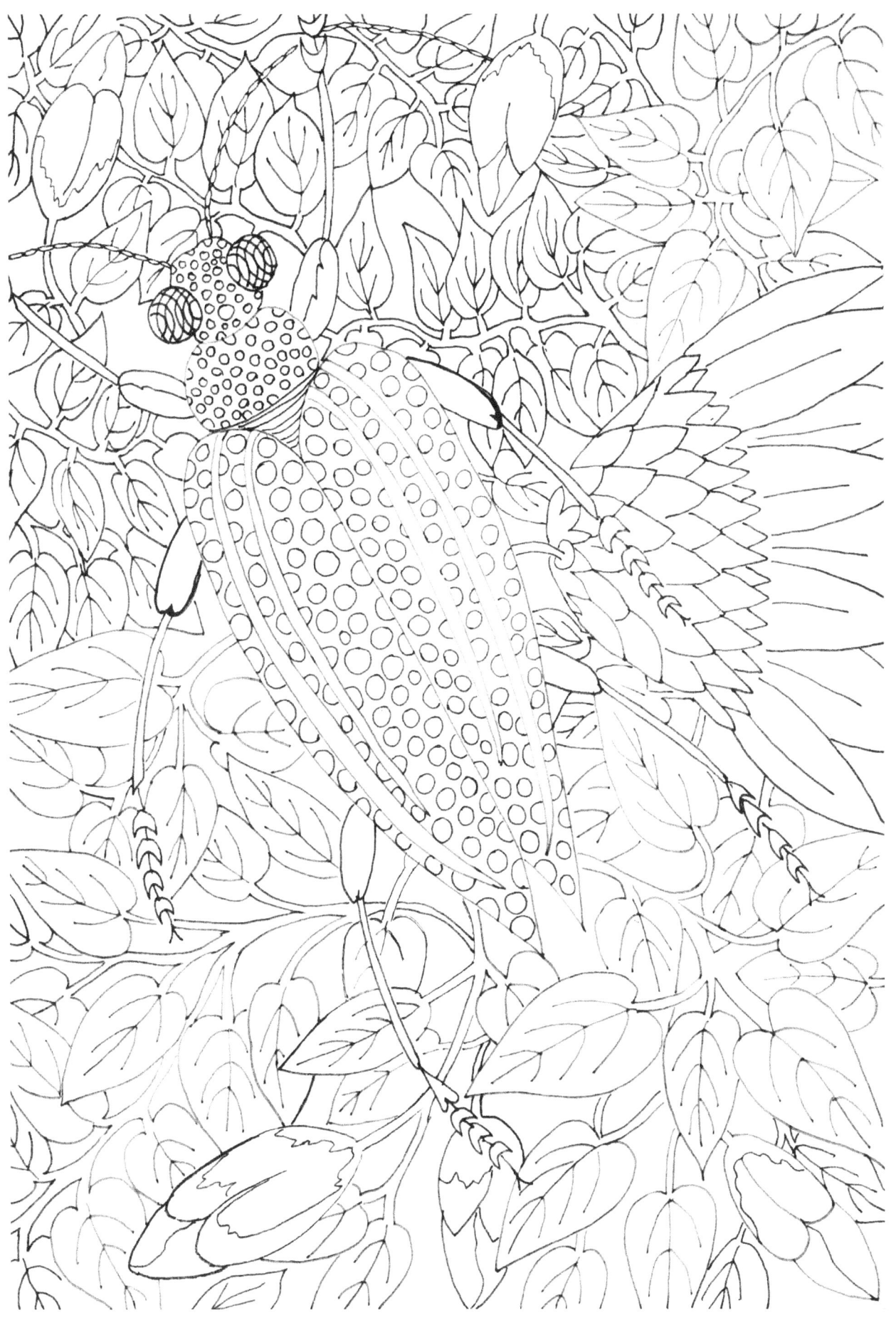

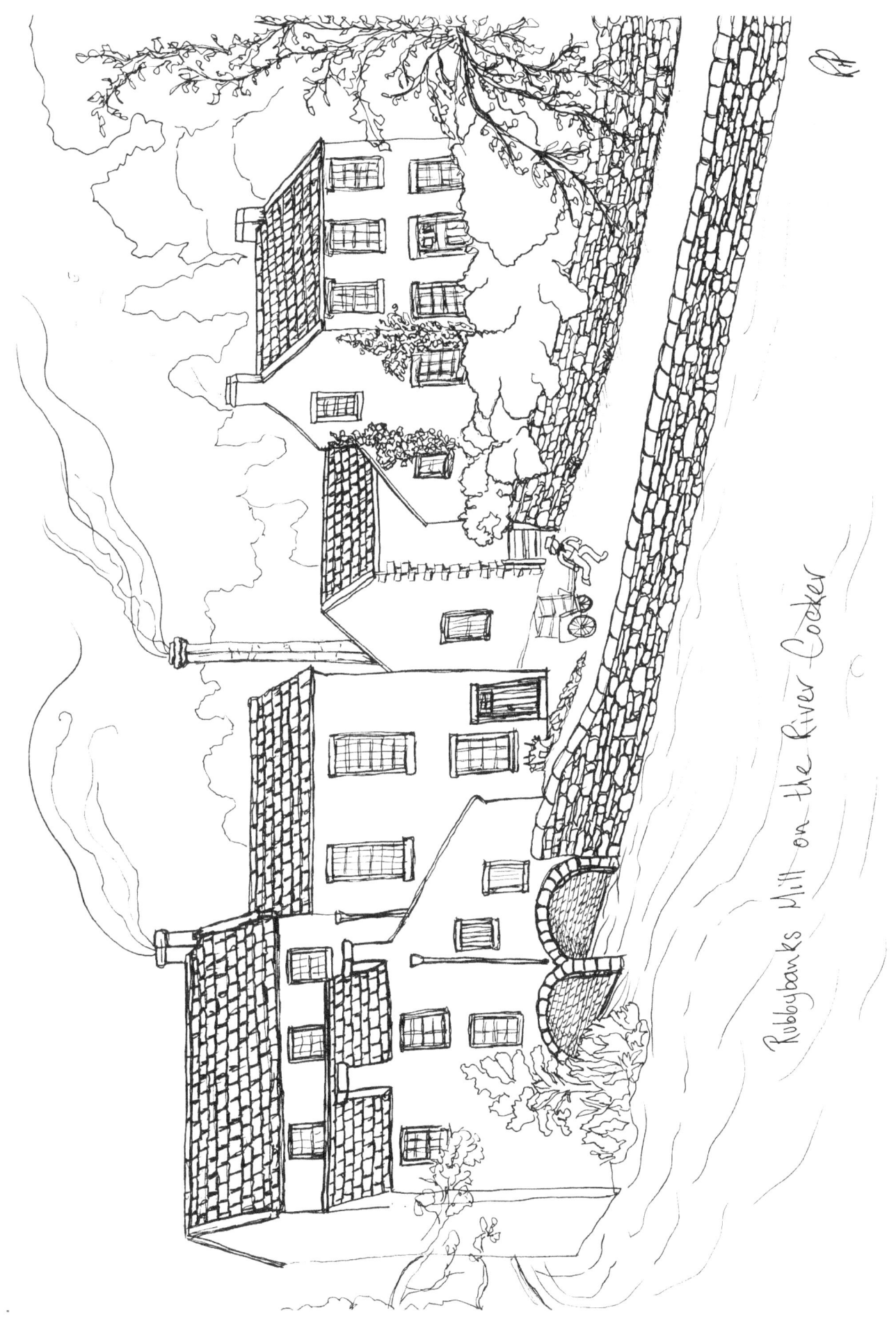

Rubbybanks Mill on the River Cocker

Rosalind Pollock

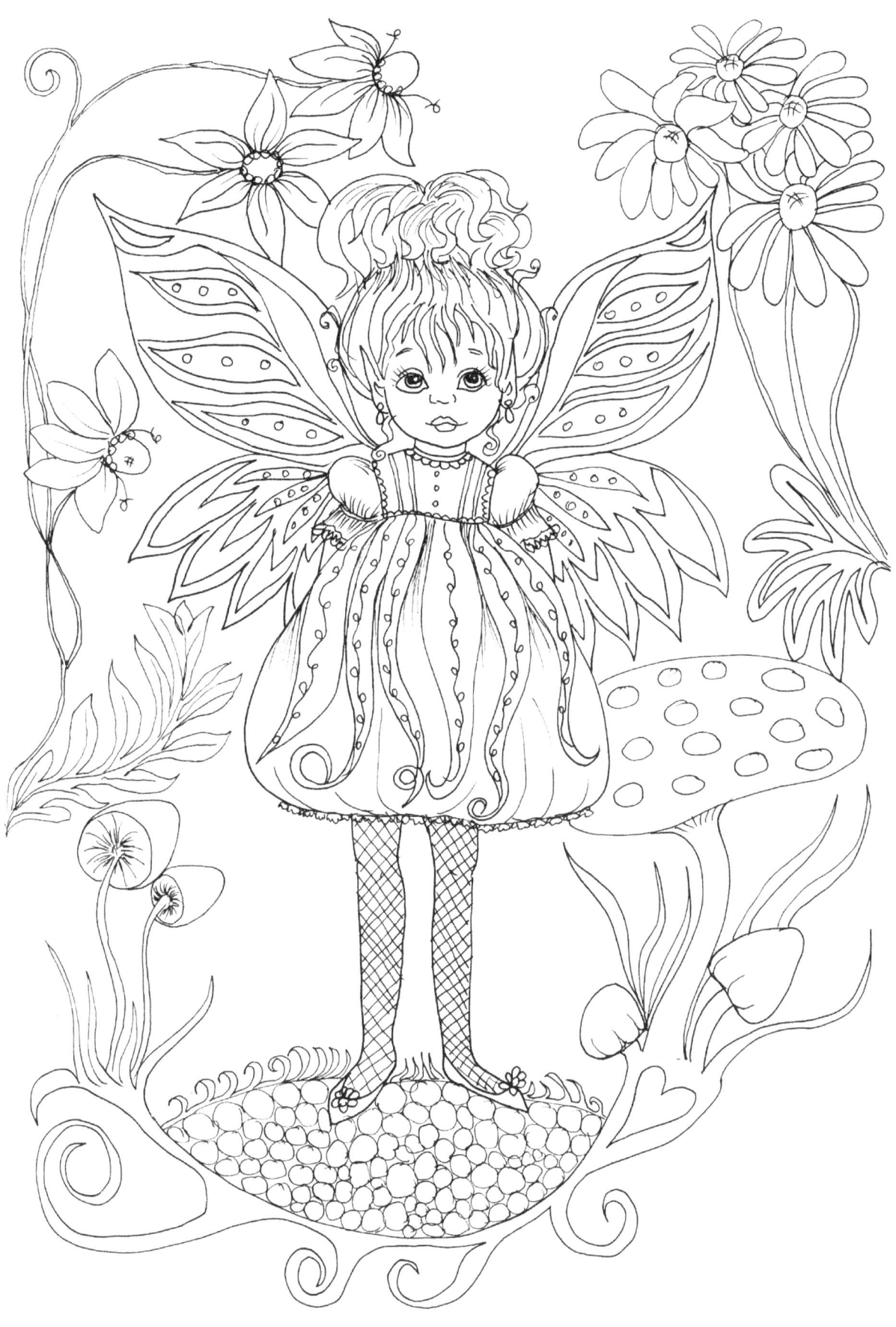

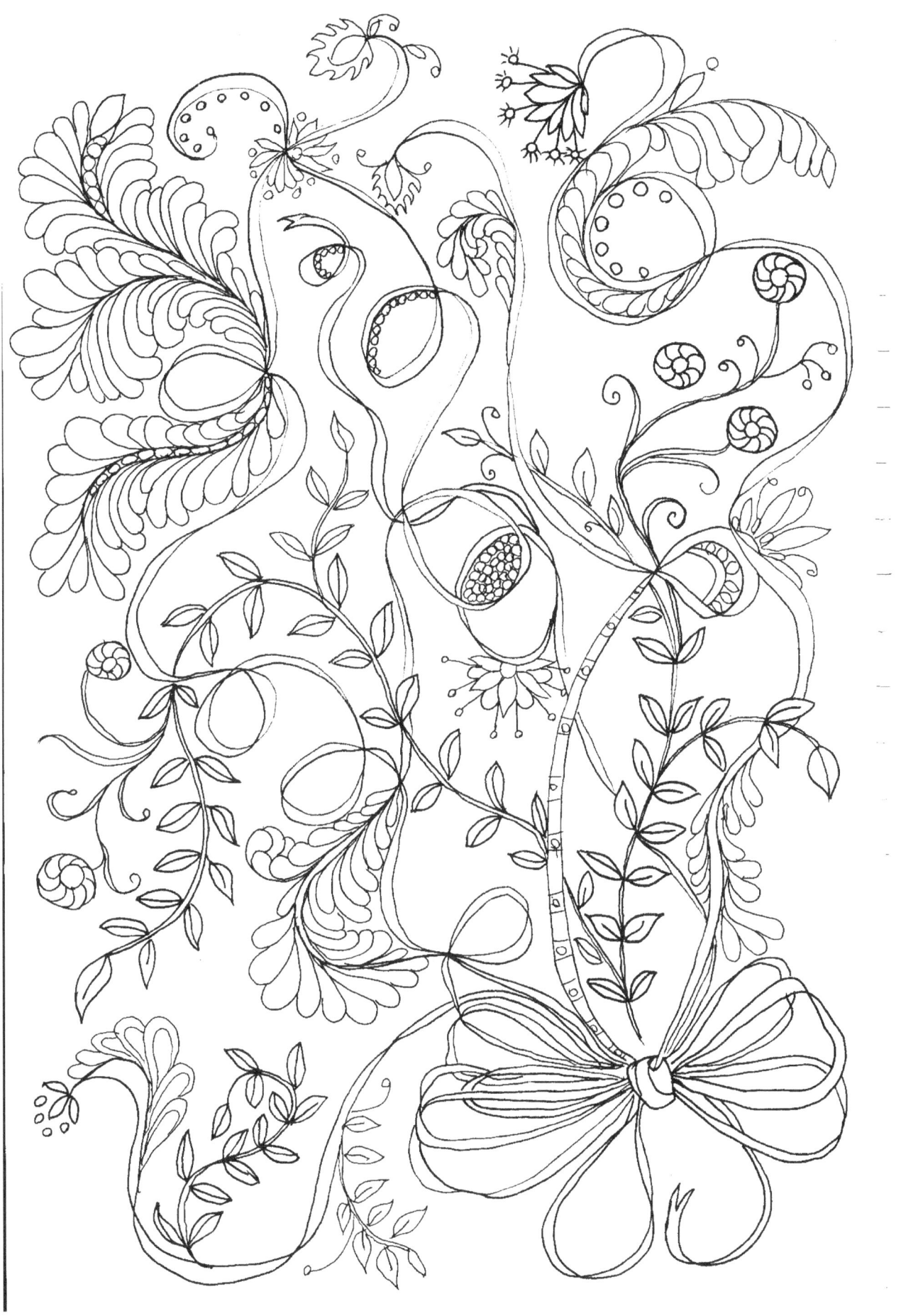

Rosalind Pollock

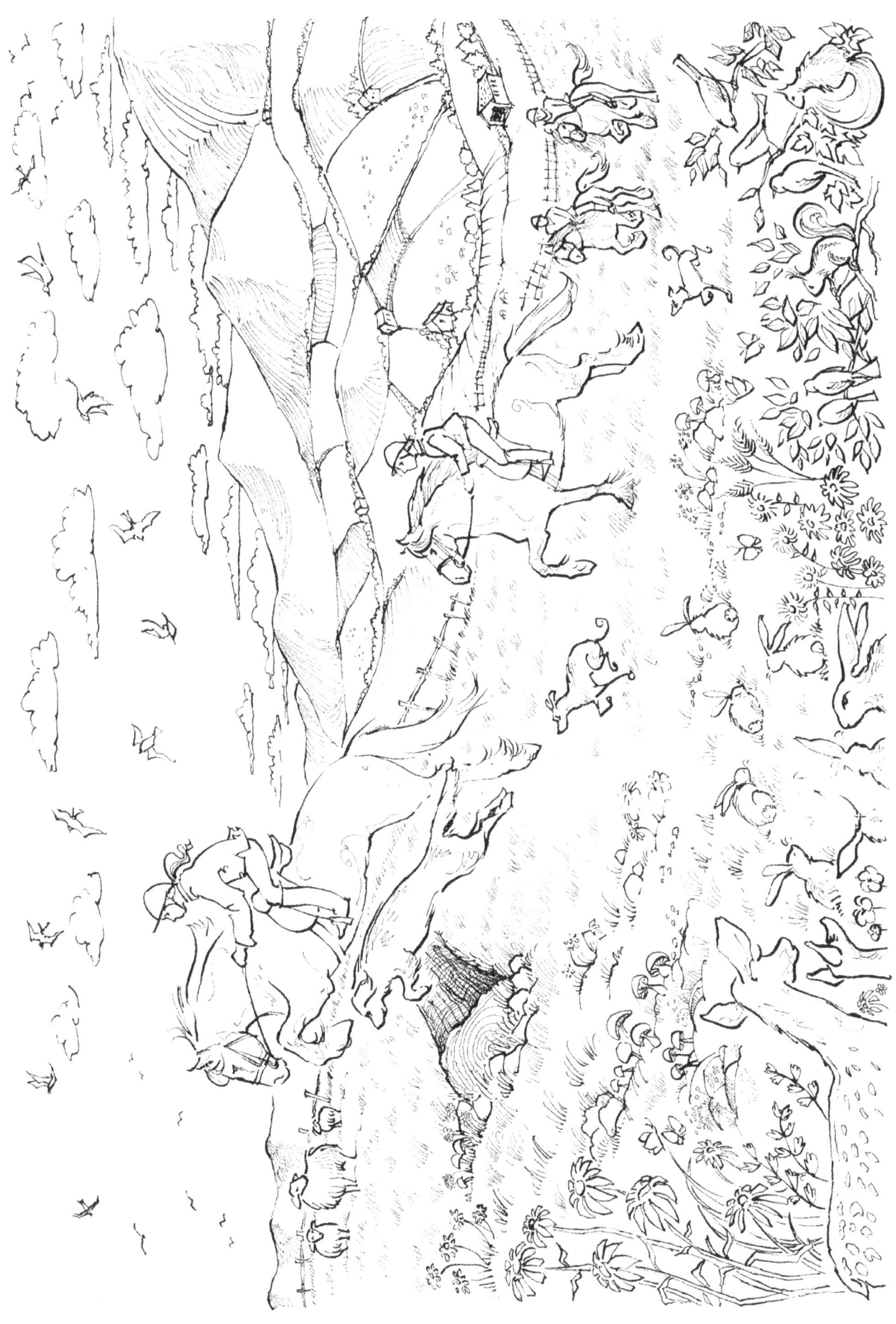

Juliet Whitworth

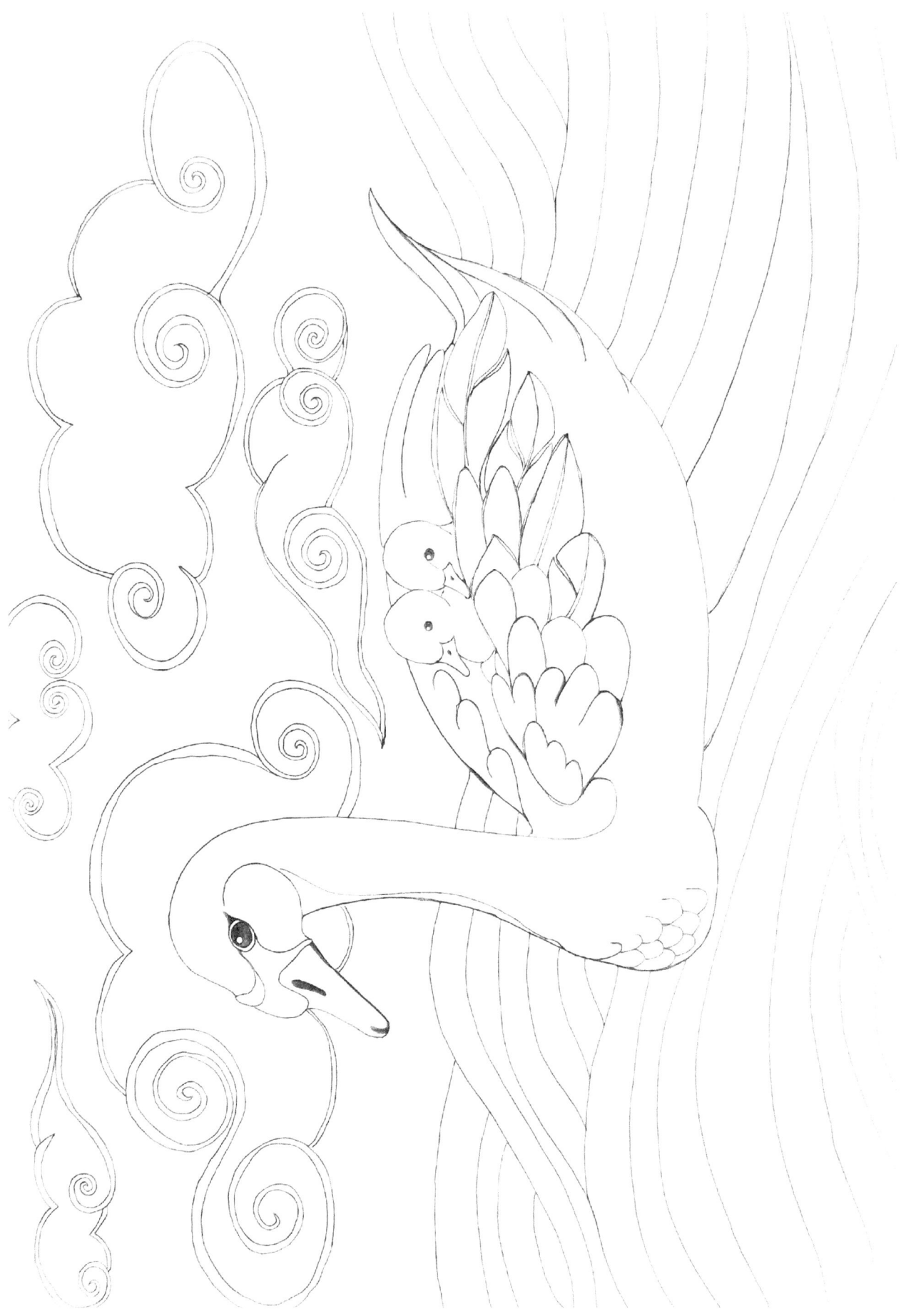

Helen Walsh

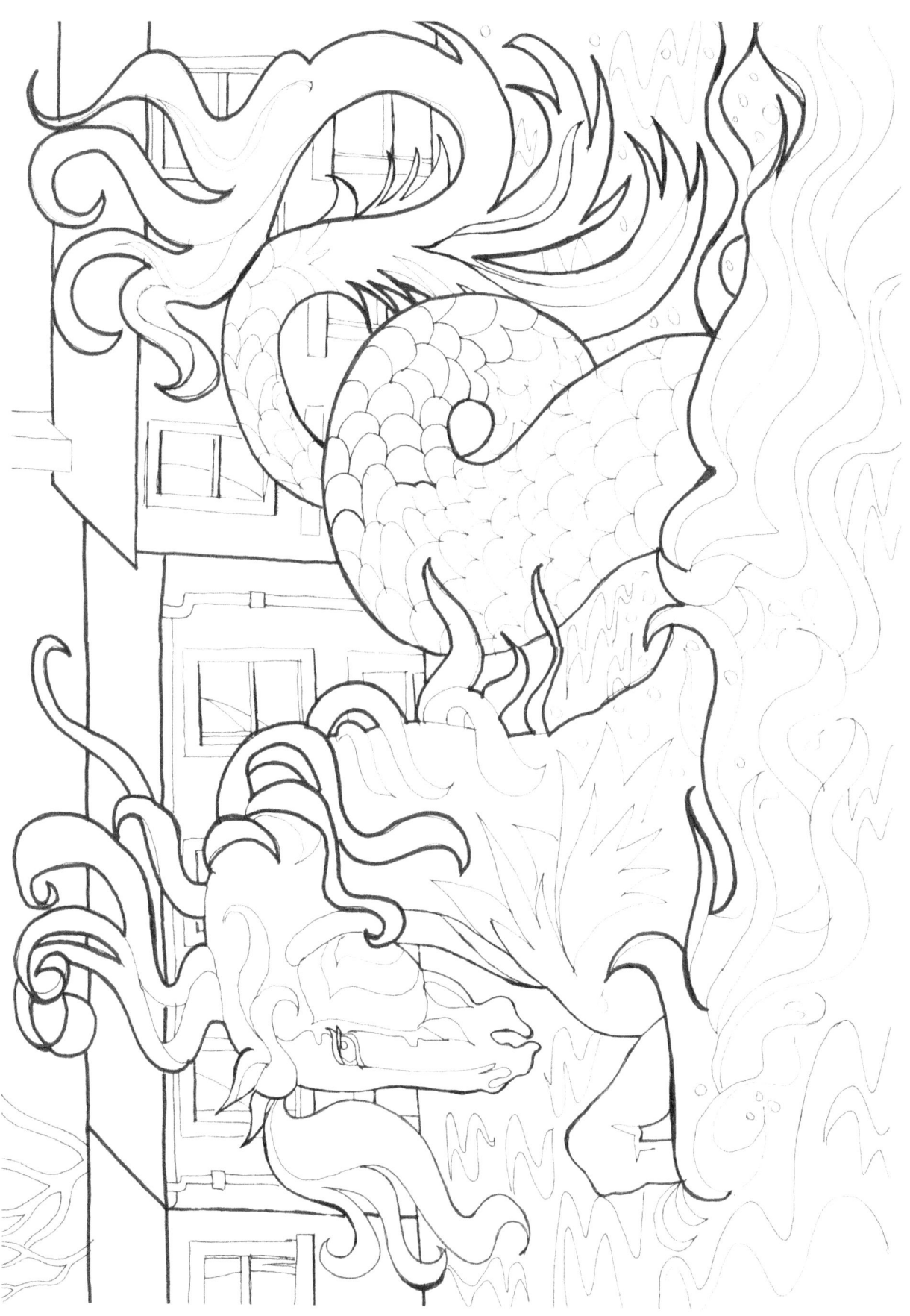

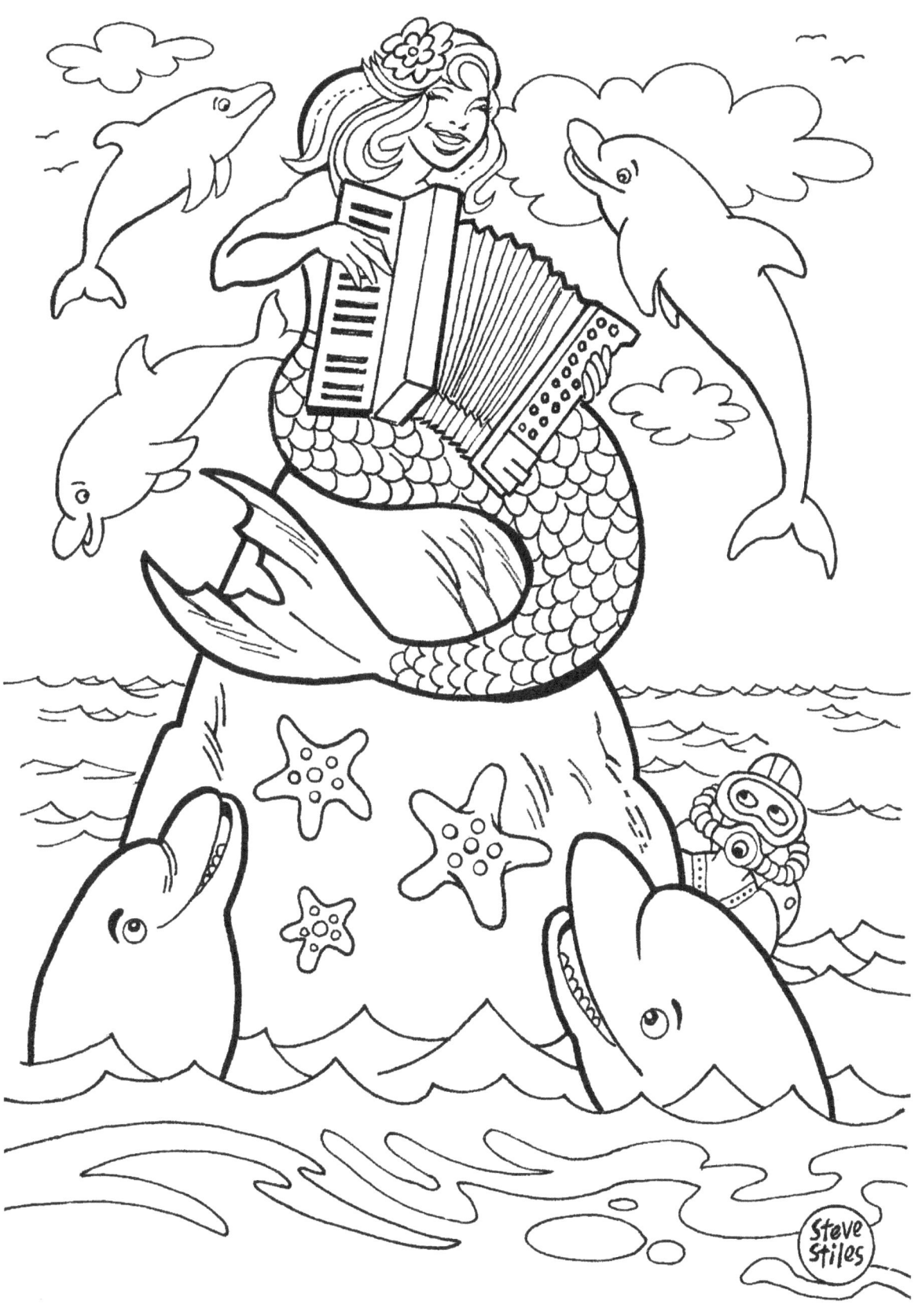

Steve Stiles

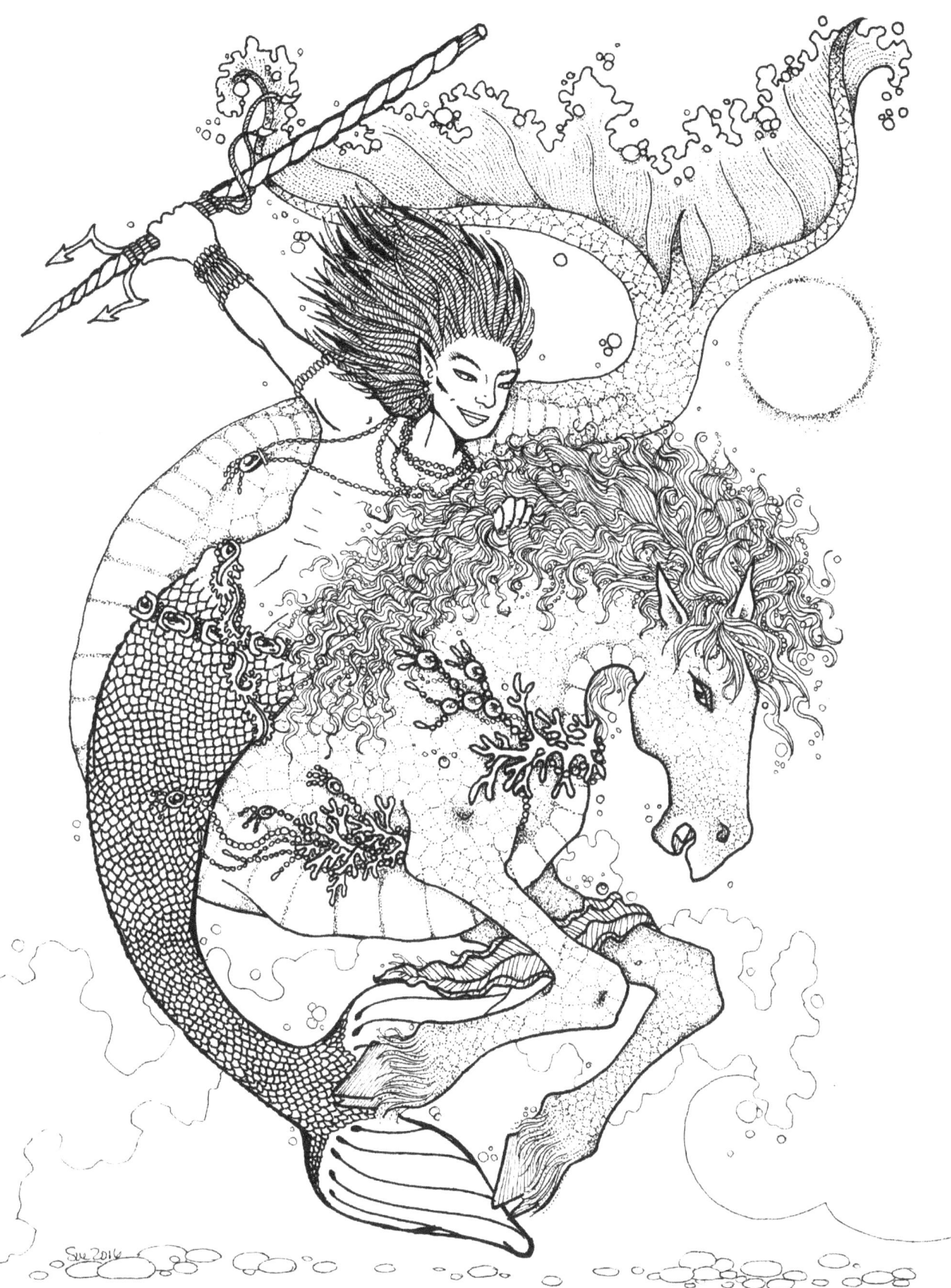

Sue Mason

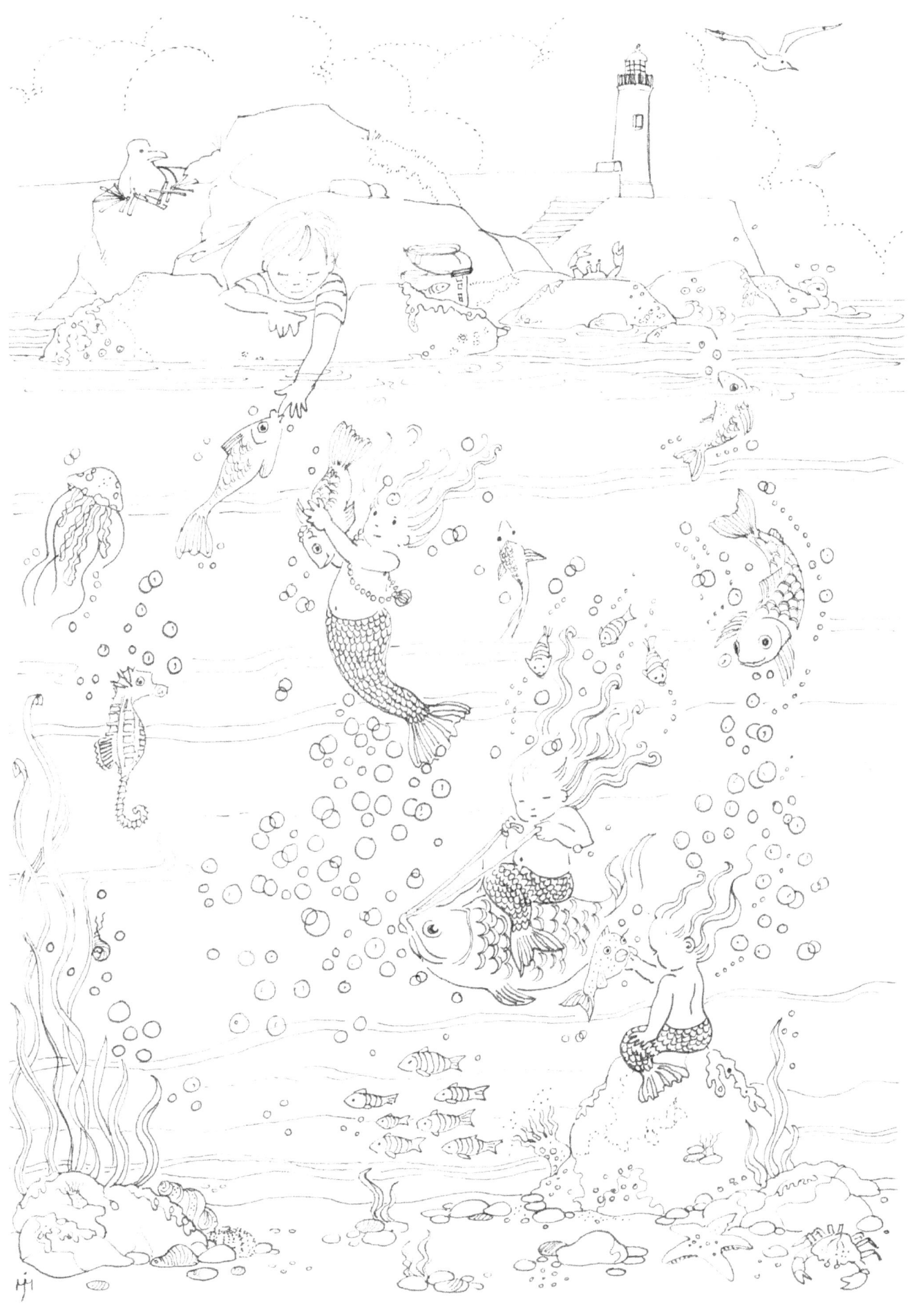

Maggie Messenger

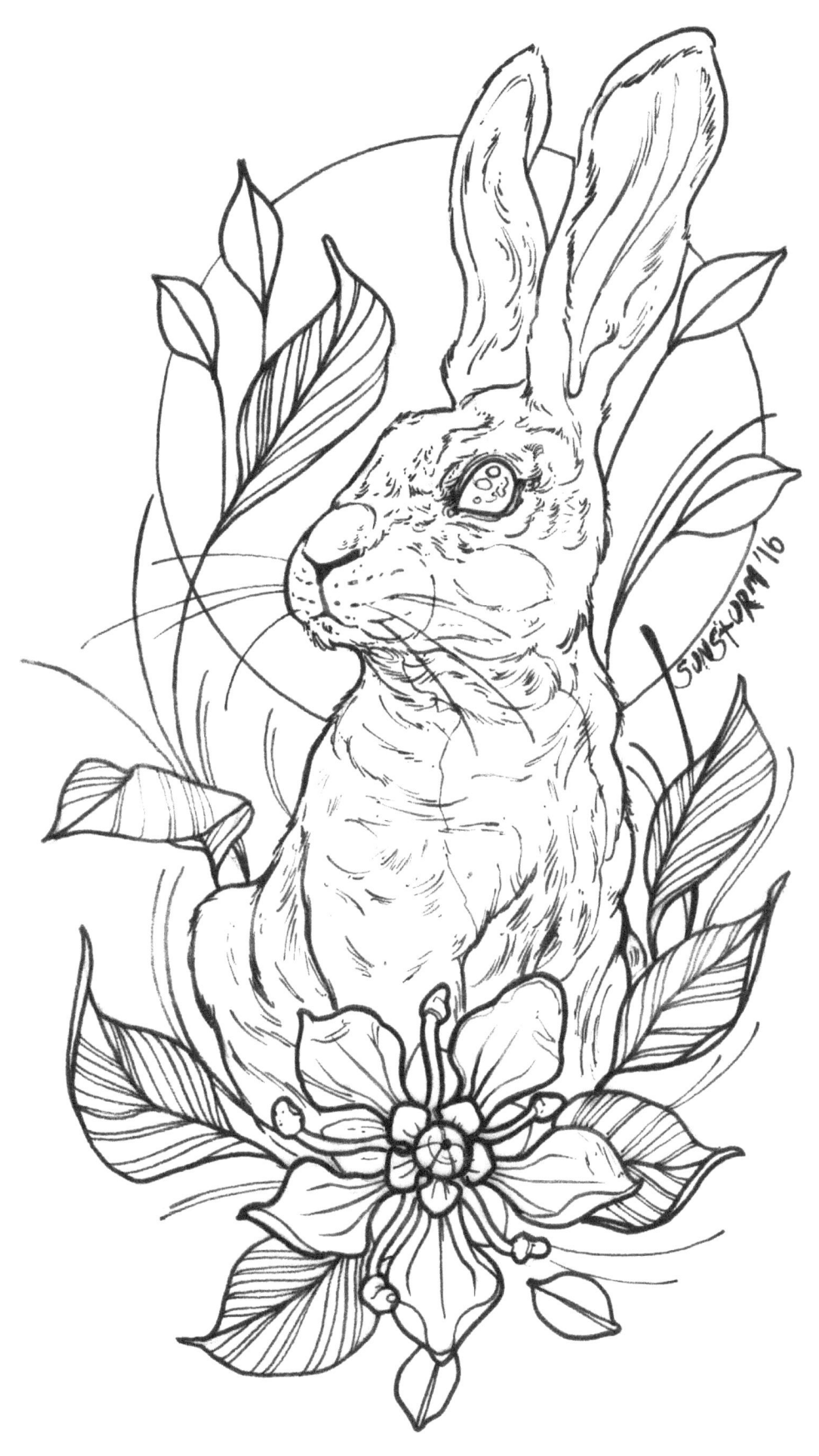

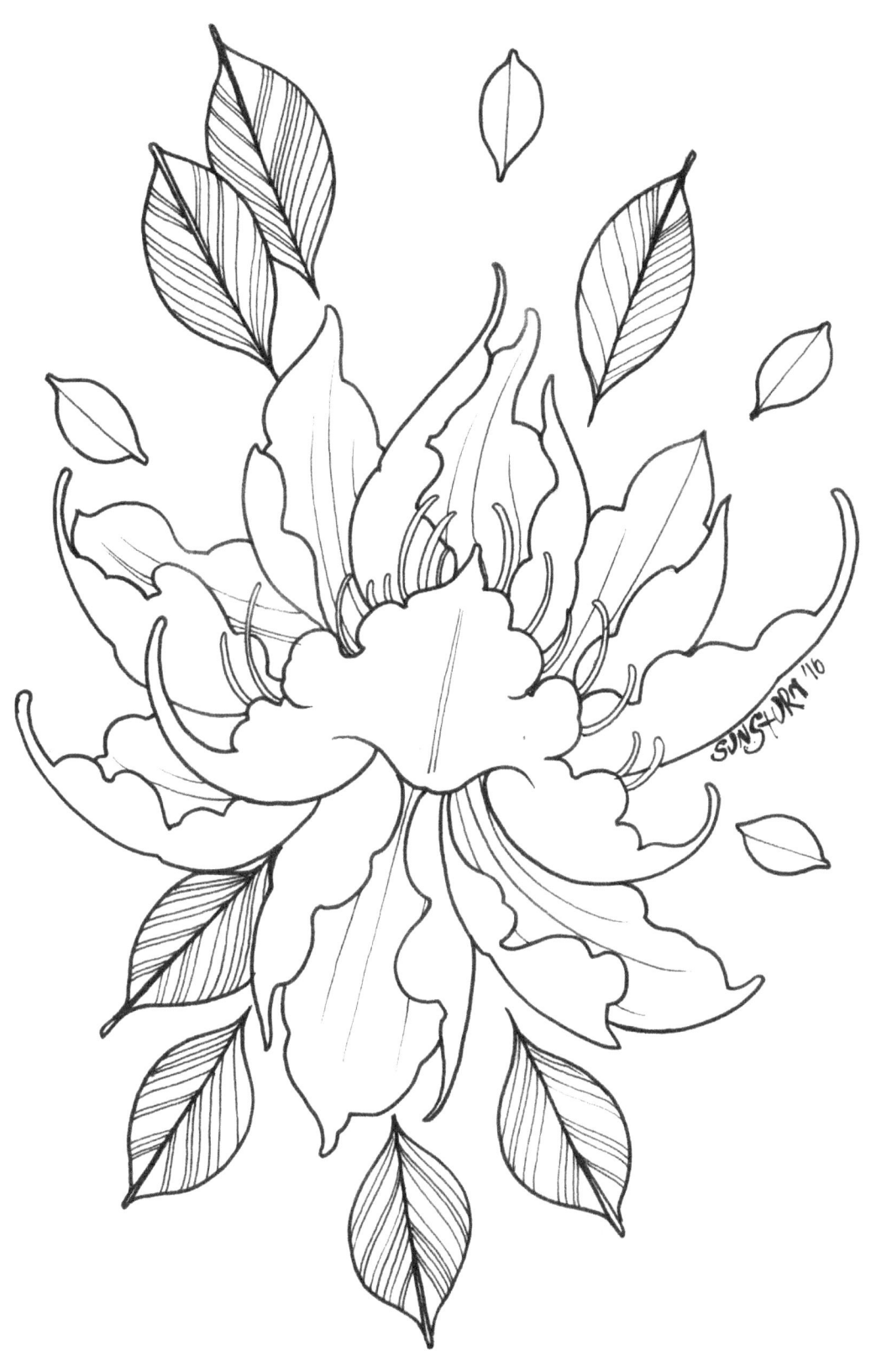

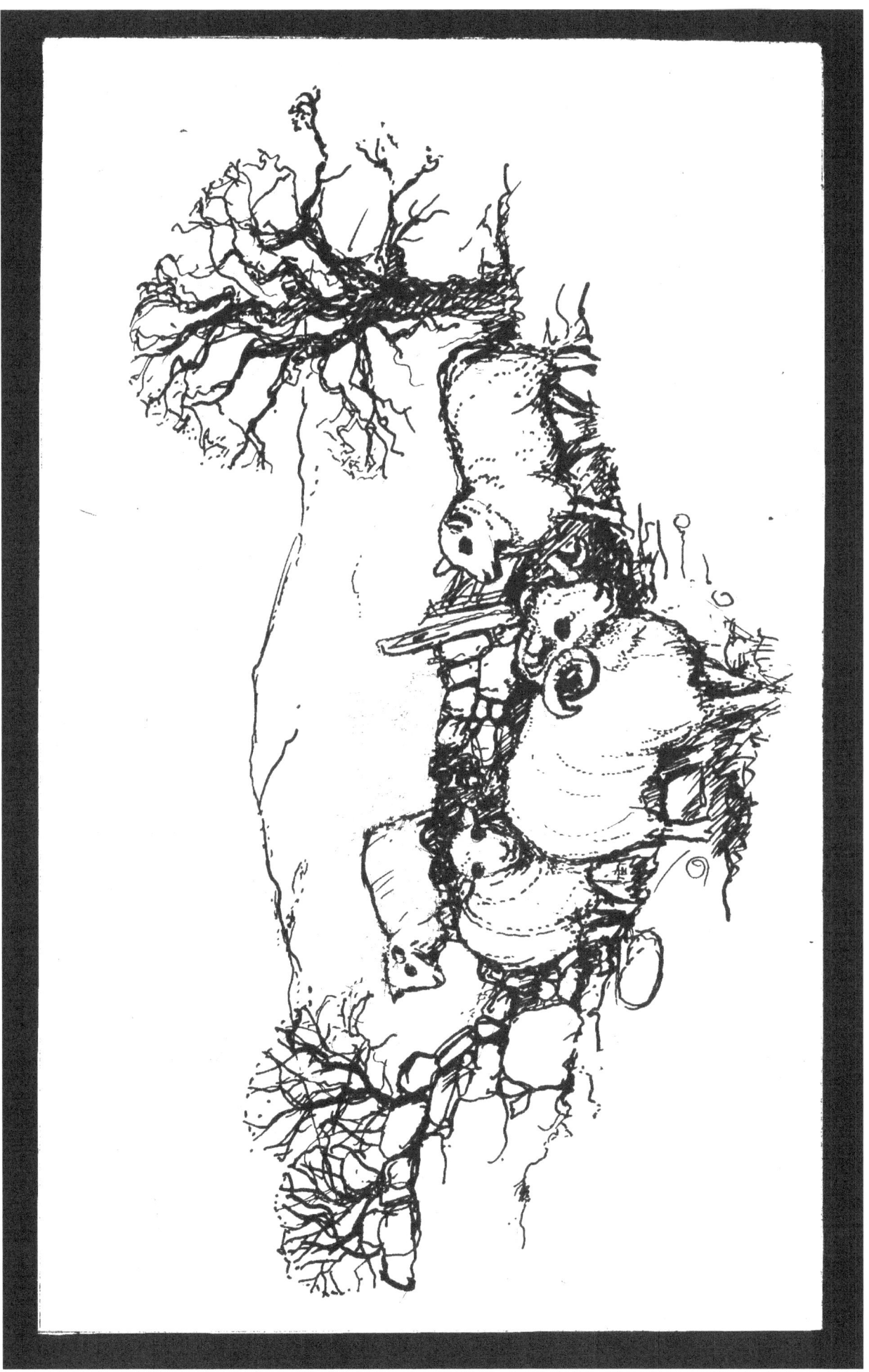

Rosetta Cowen

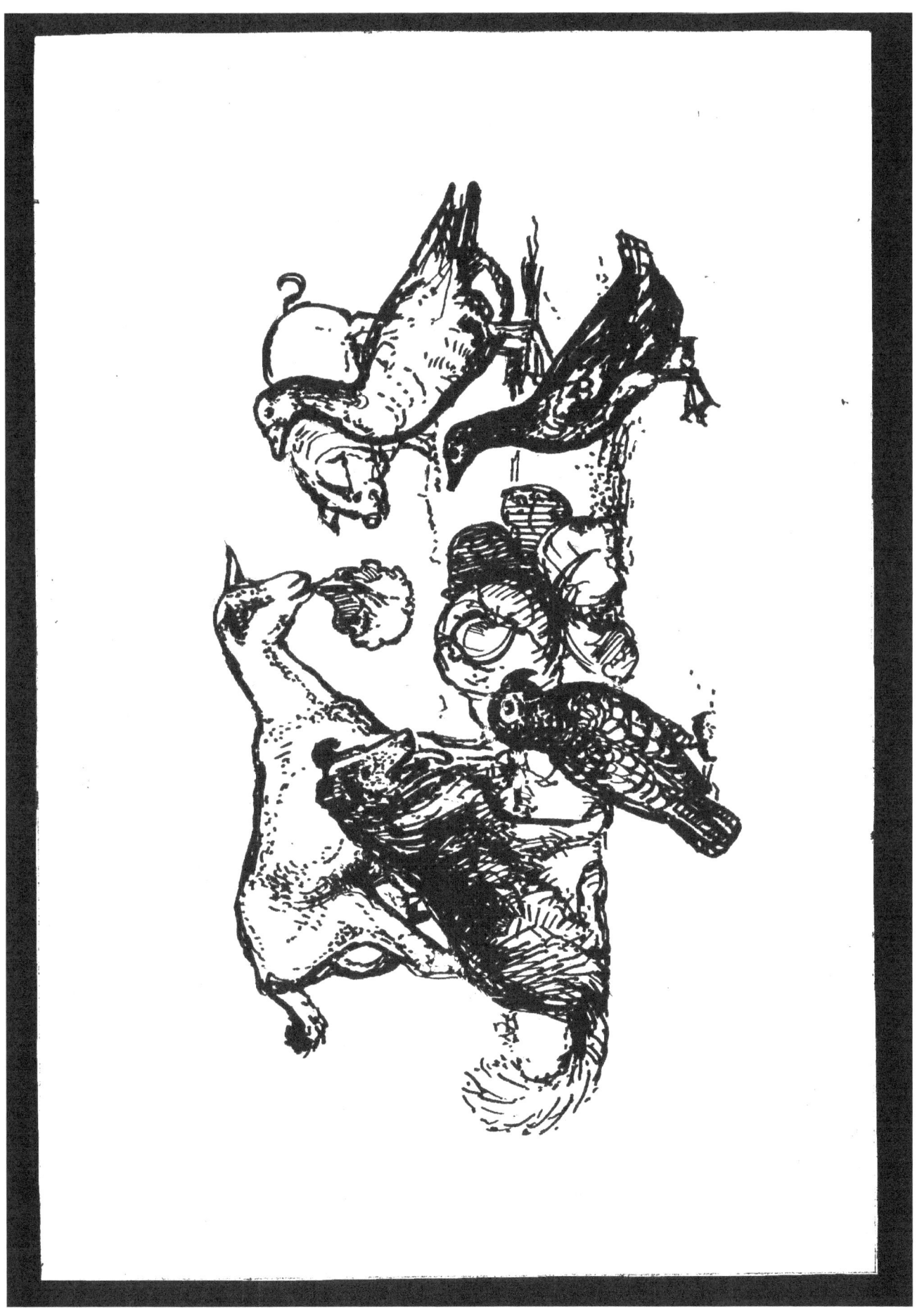

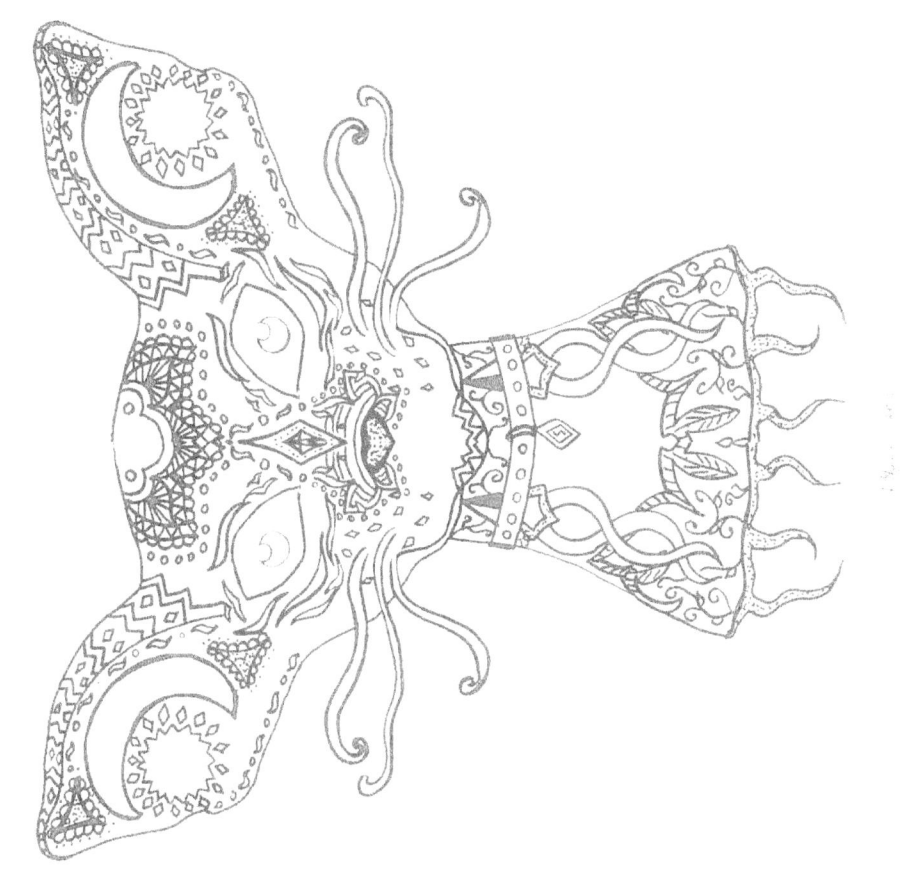

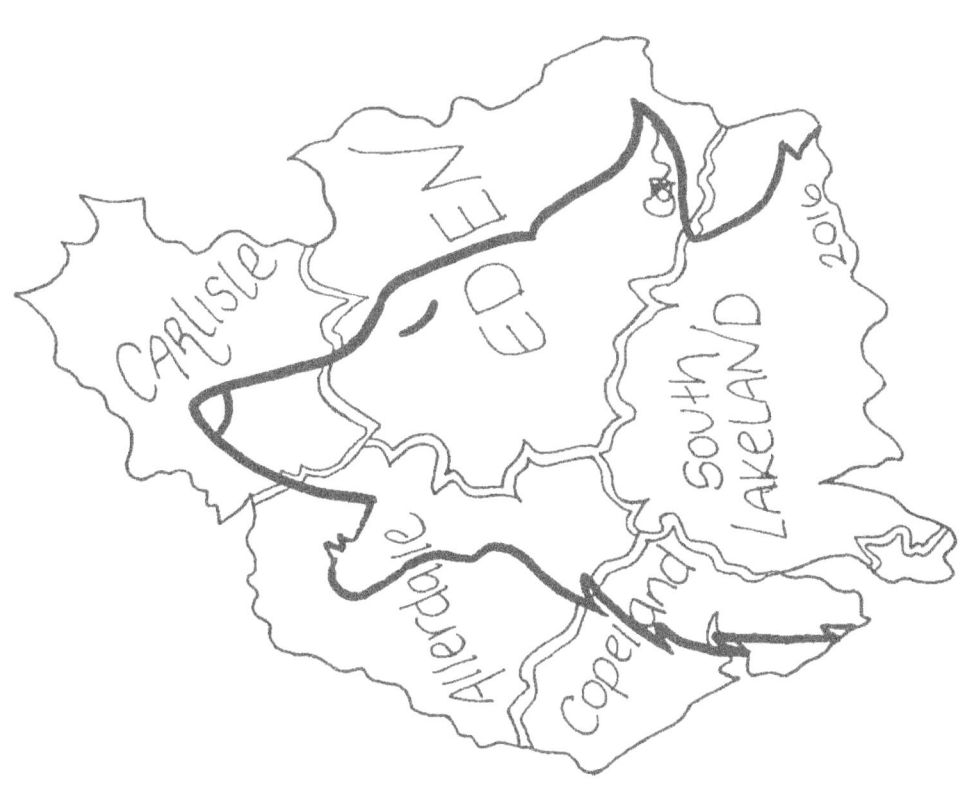

Agata

Caitlin

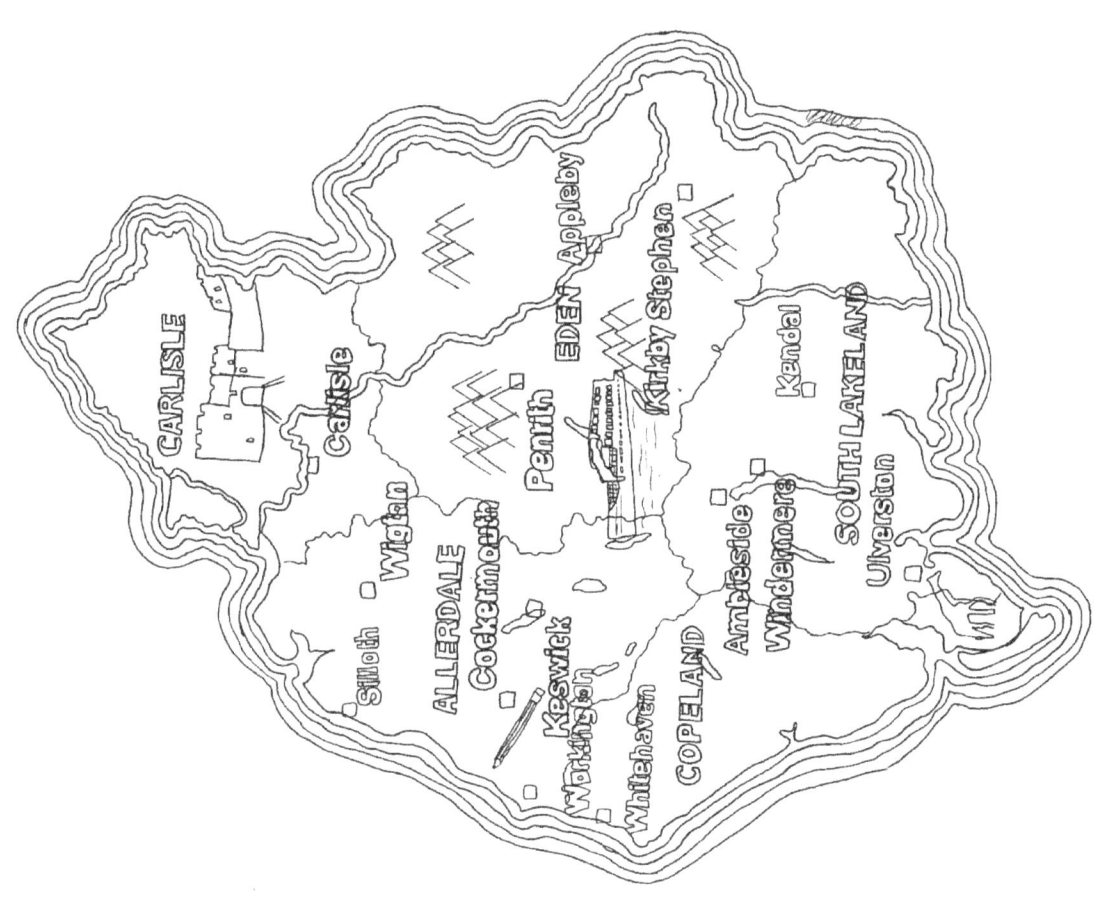

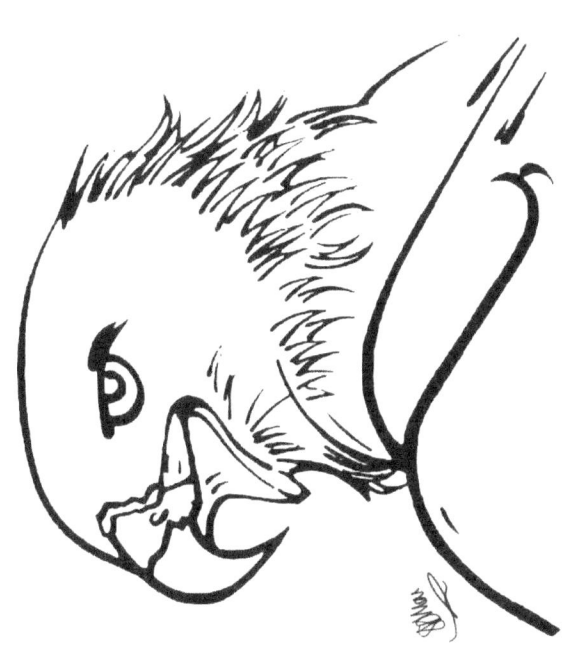

Georgia

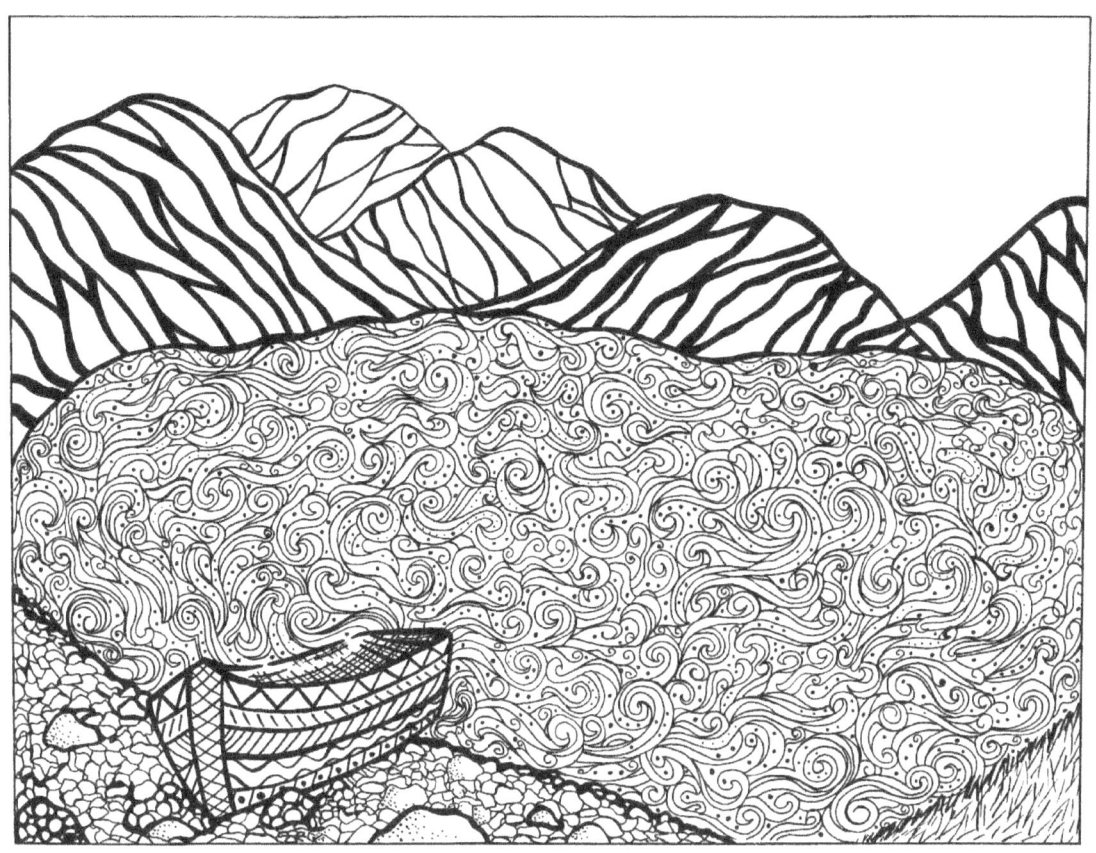

E. Halliburton

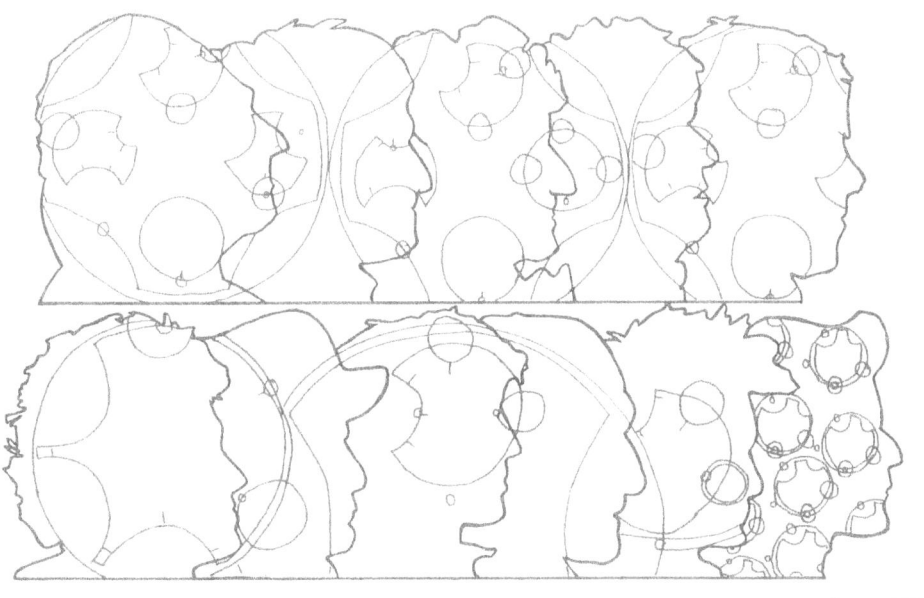

Scubber 5.02.16

Emma

Stevie

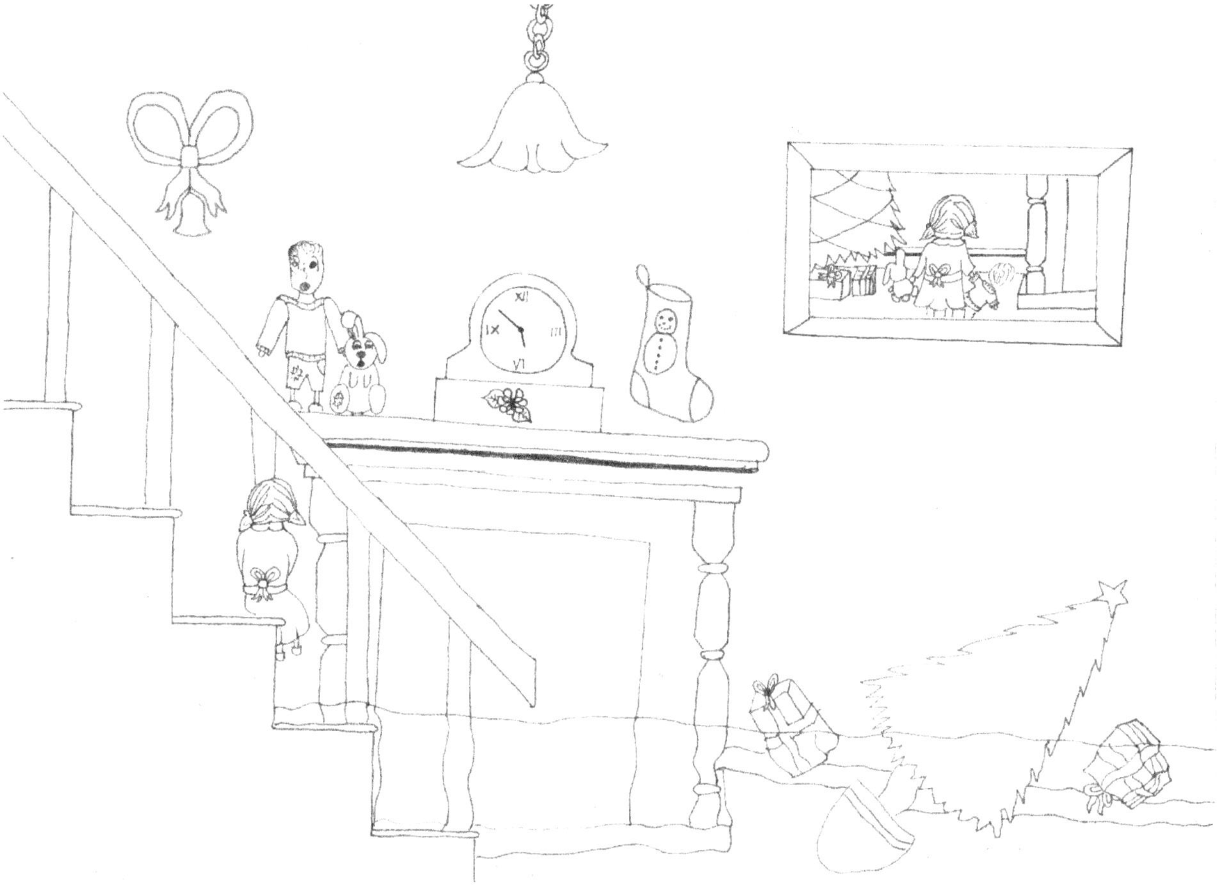

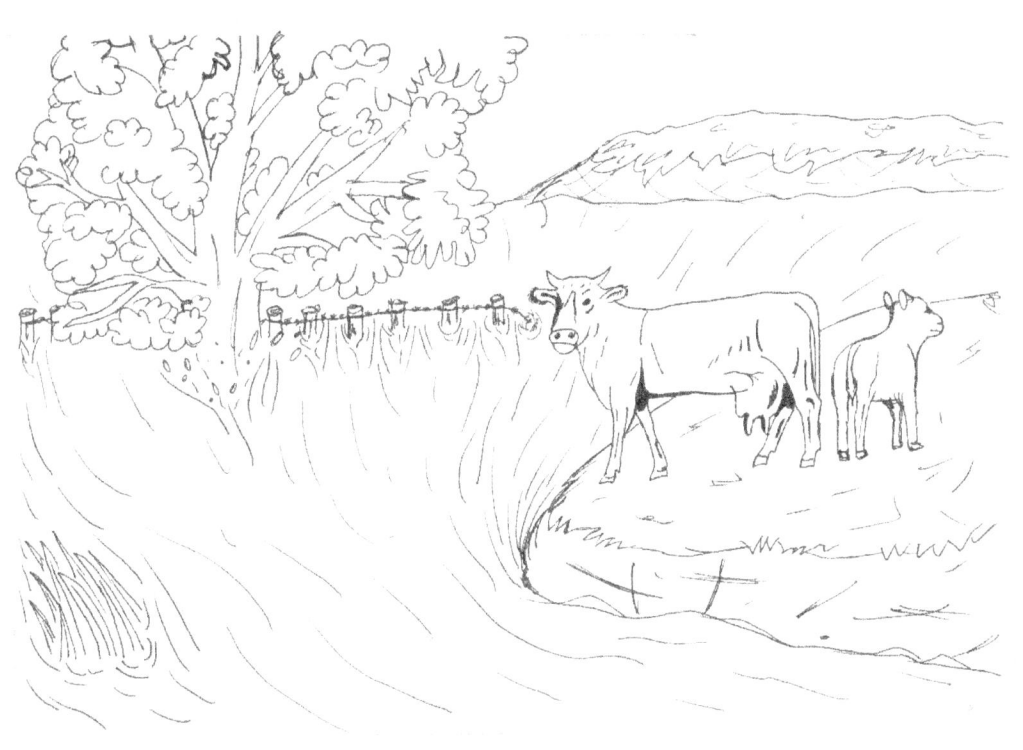

JASMINE CAMPBELL FLYNN / QEGS / Year 9 / 14

Tanya Culmore QEGS


Jasmine Campbell  Flynn QEGS

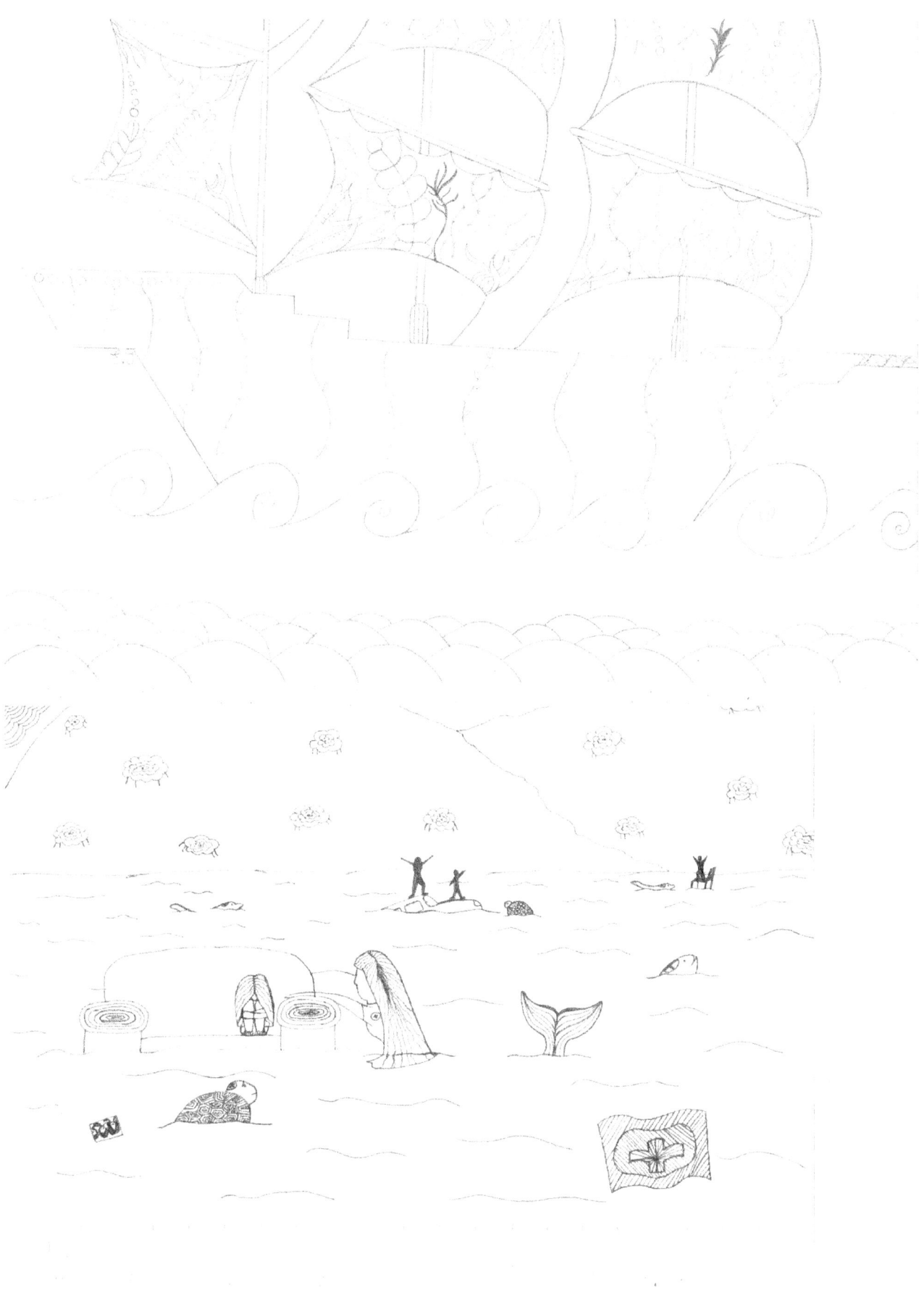

Eleanor Joyce QEGS

Chloe Parsons QEGS

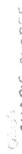

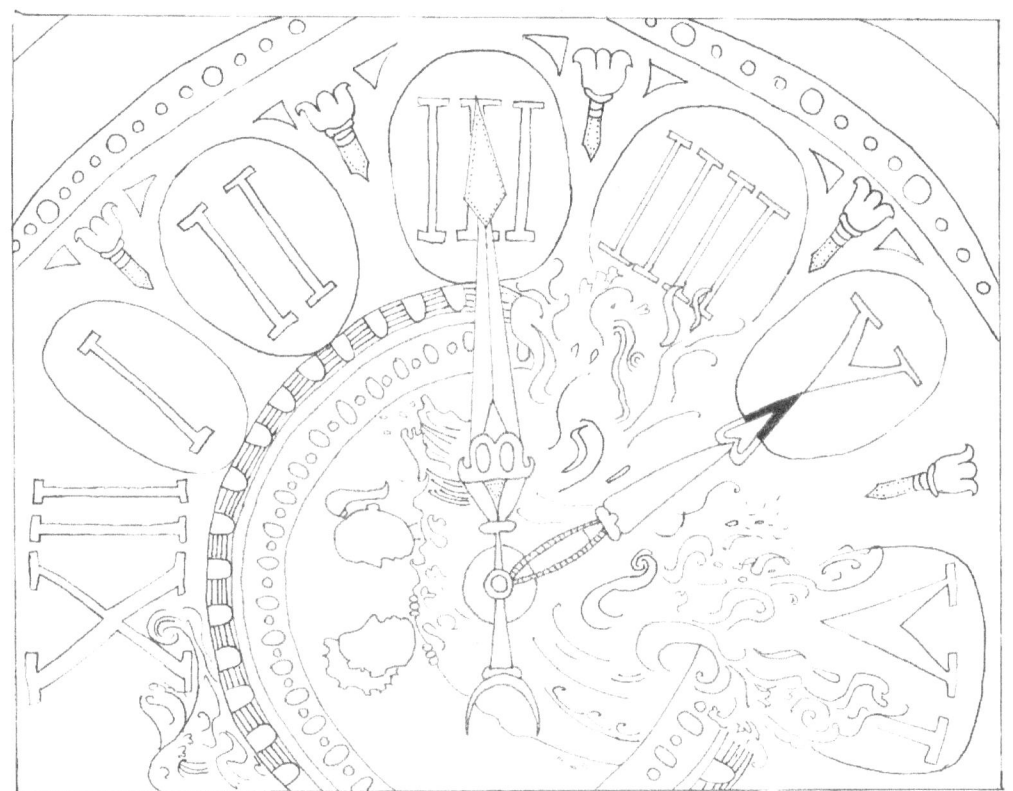

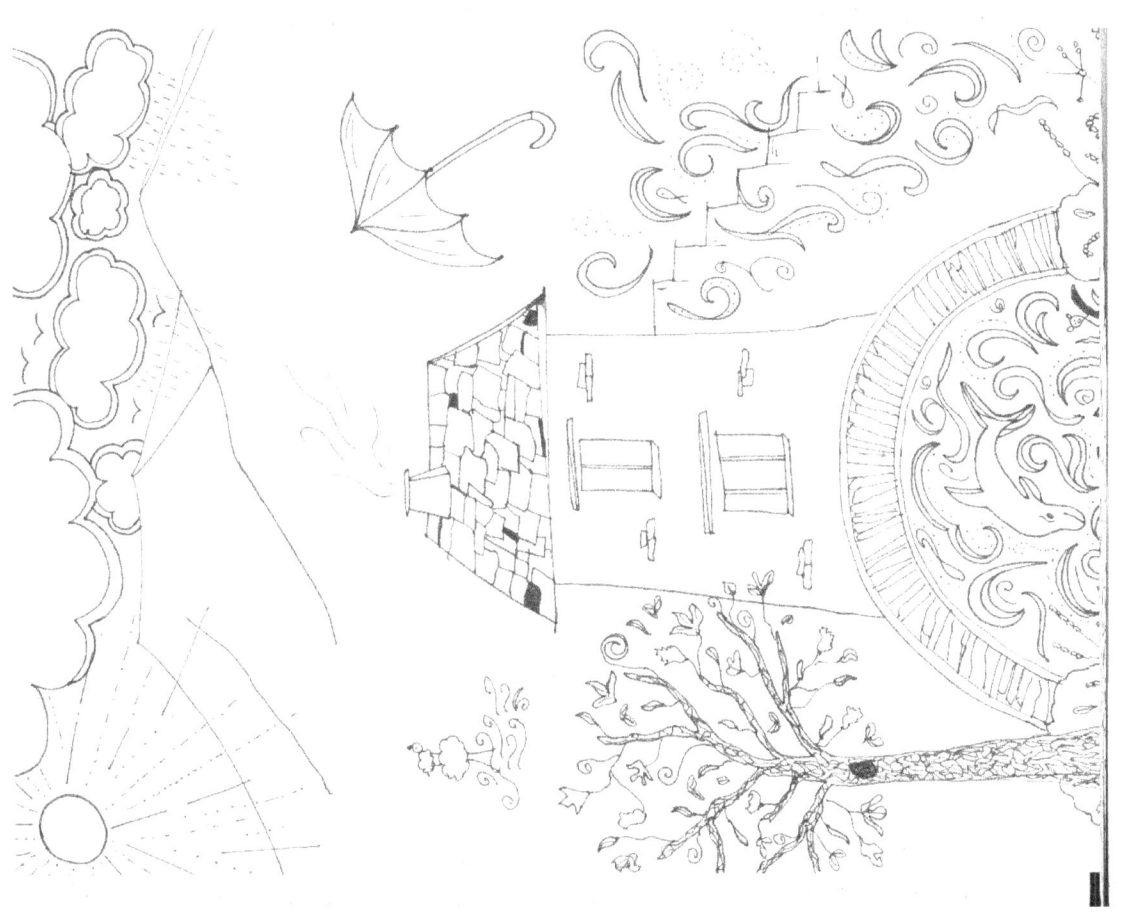

Charis Rhodes QEGS

Rebecca  Ironmonger QEGS

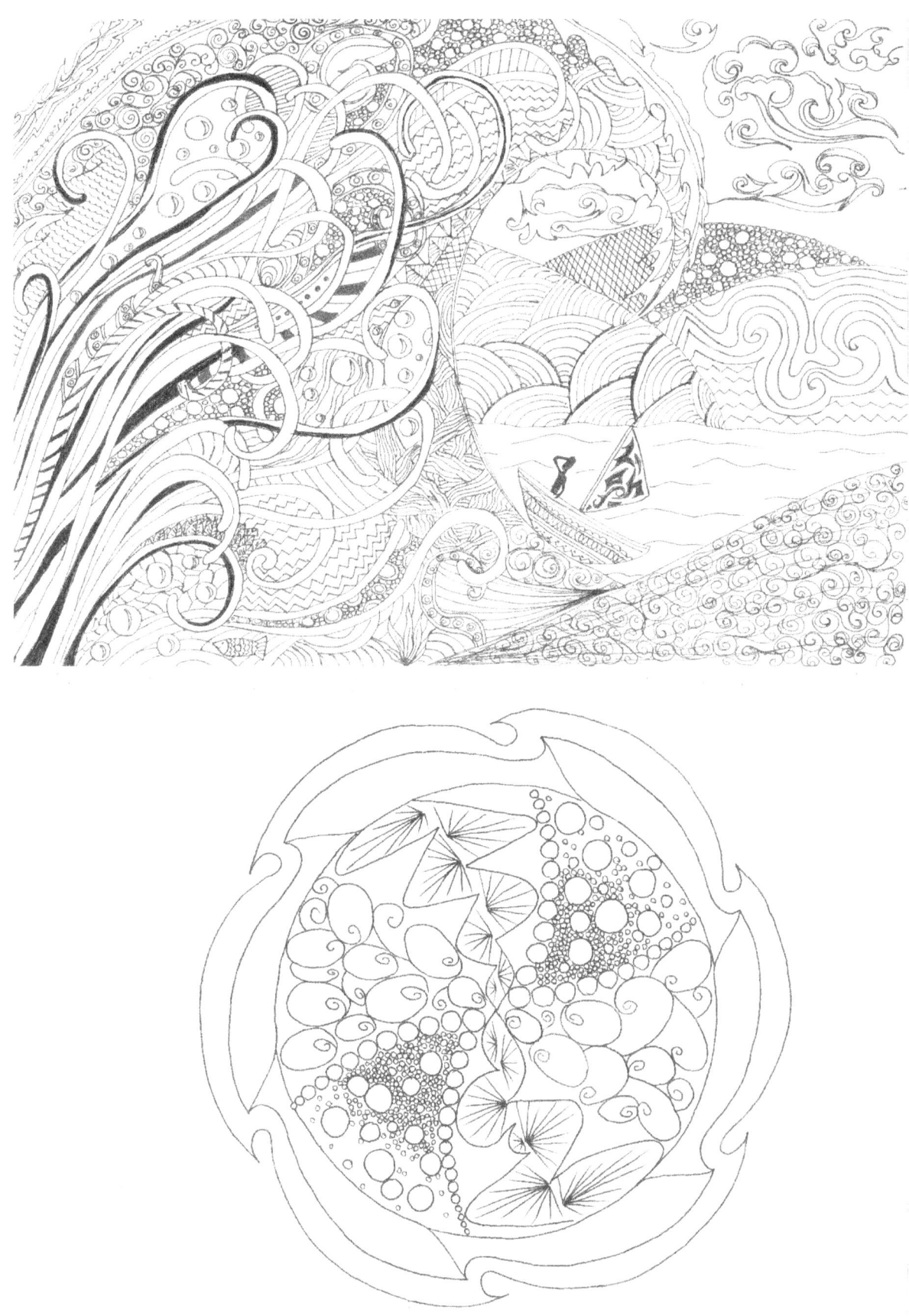

Esme Chan  QEGS

Imogen Rolfe QEGS

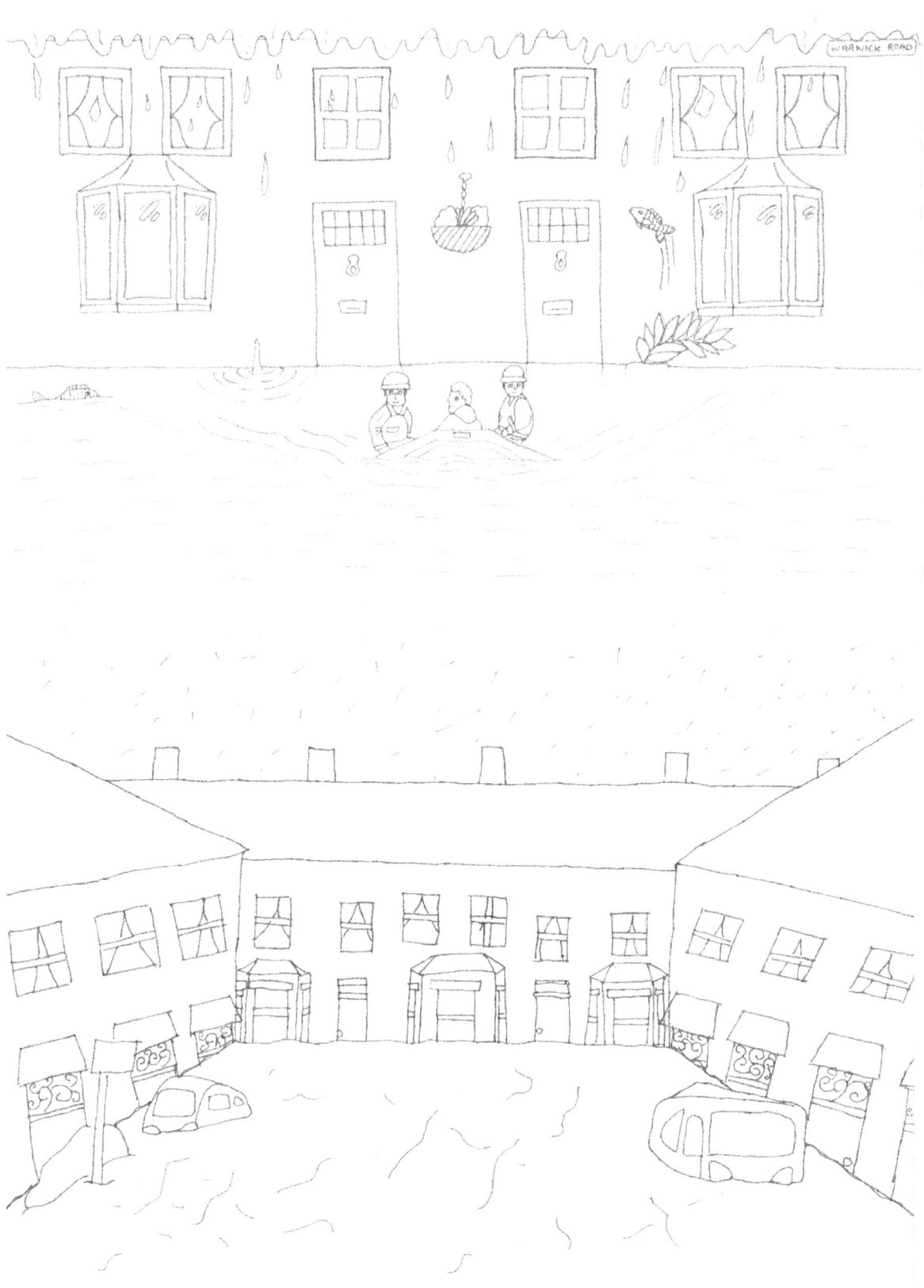

Adelka Valentova QEGS

Rhiannon Cullen QEGS

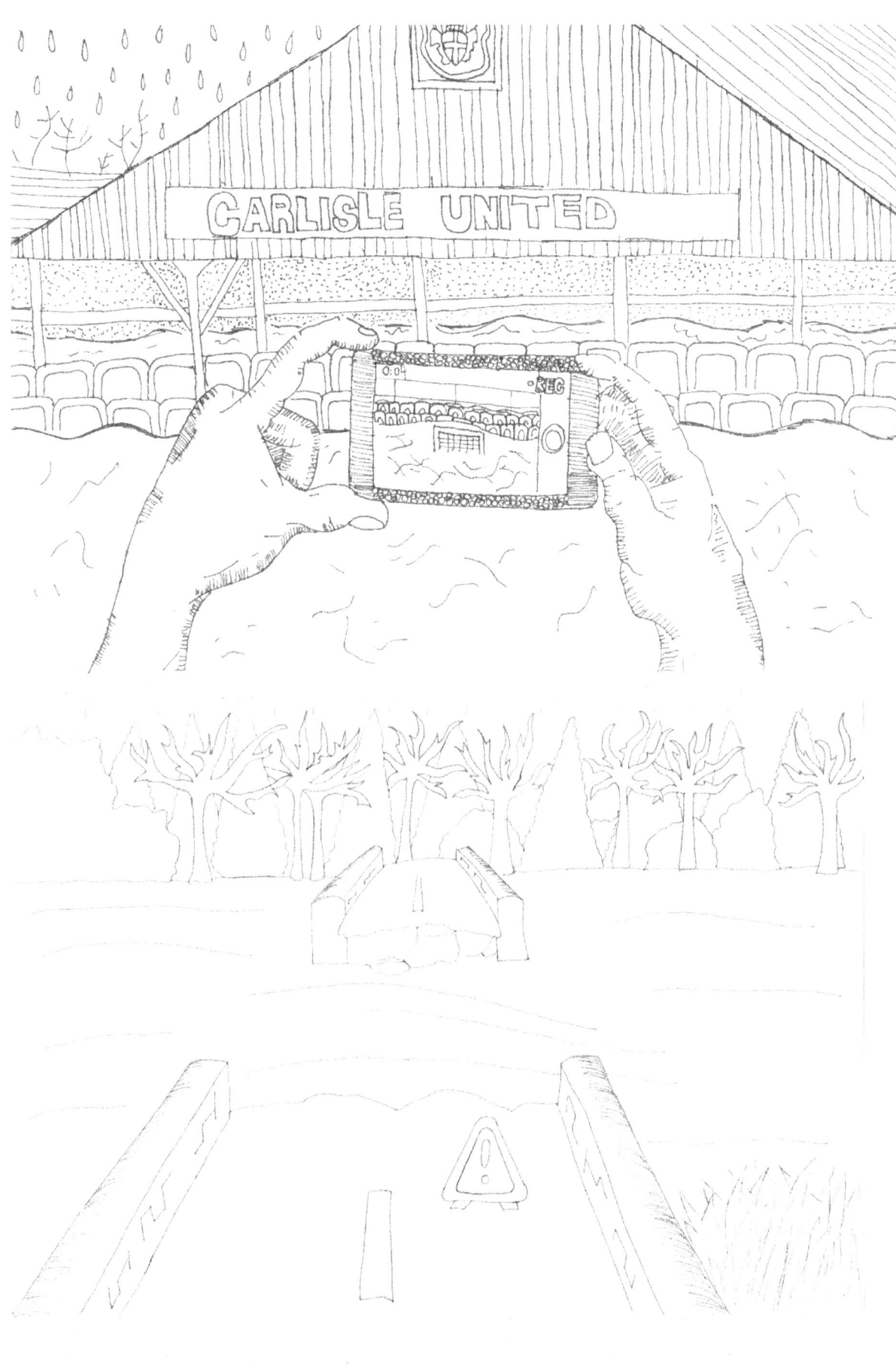

Tia Johnston QEGS

Lois Whitfield QEGS

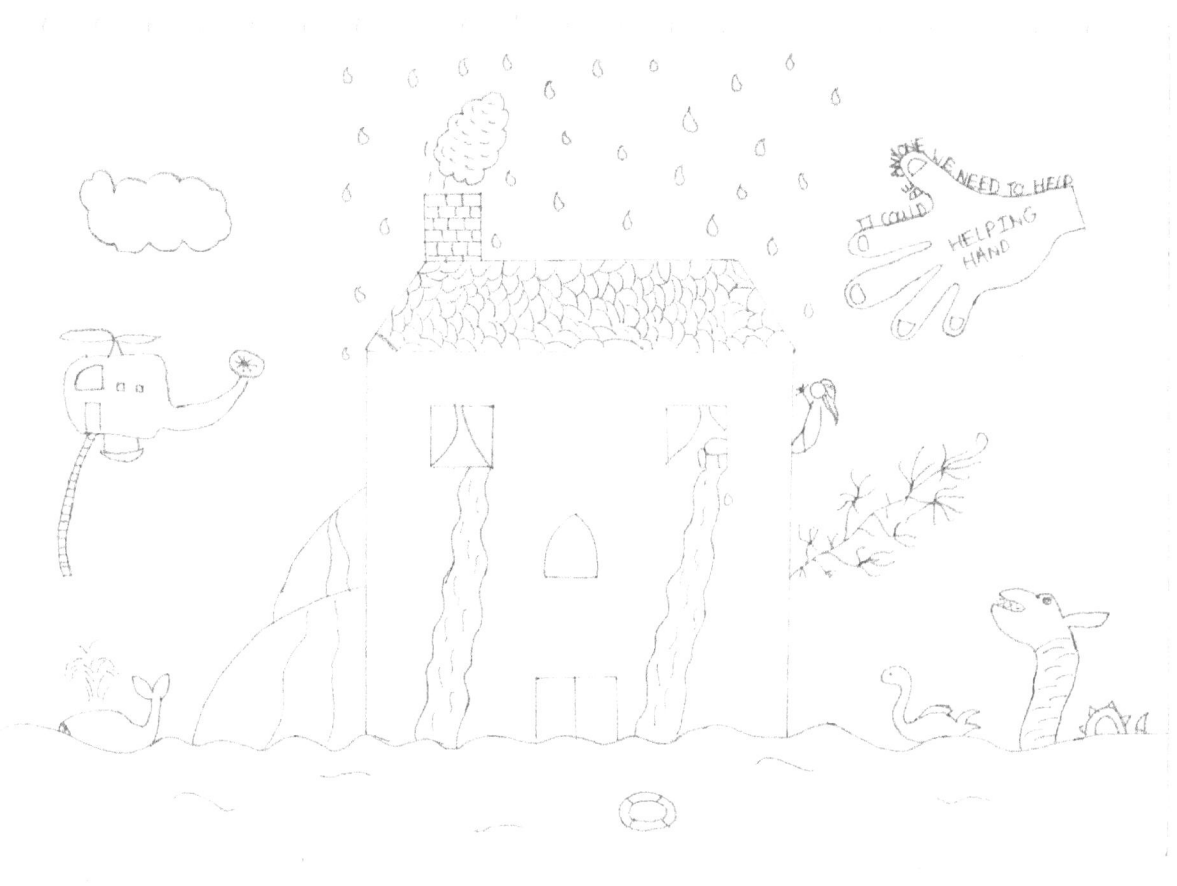

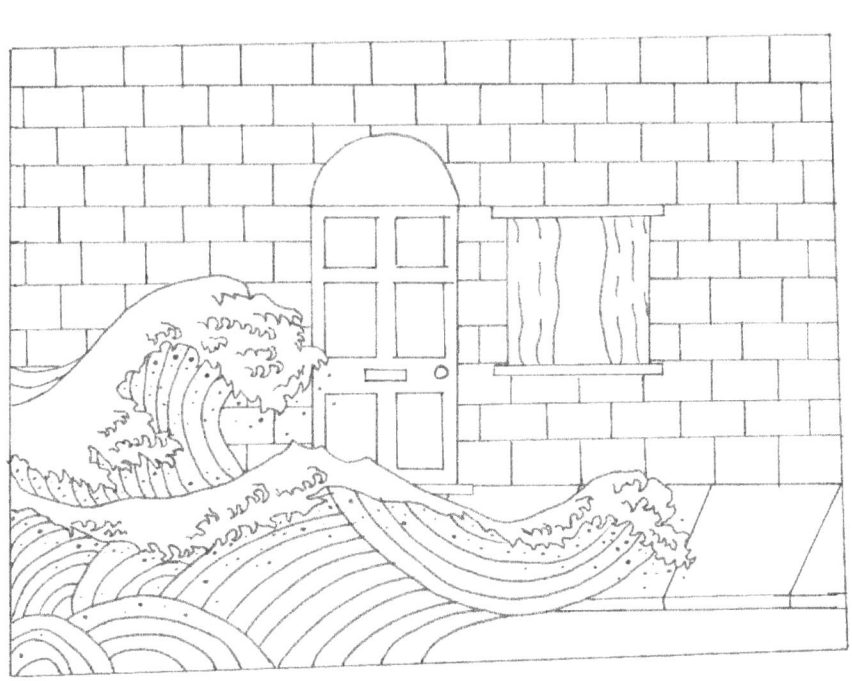

Alisha Haynes Cae Yr3 Age 13

Han Cheng Liu QEGS

Alisha Haines QEGS

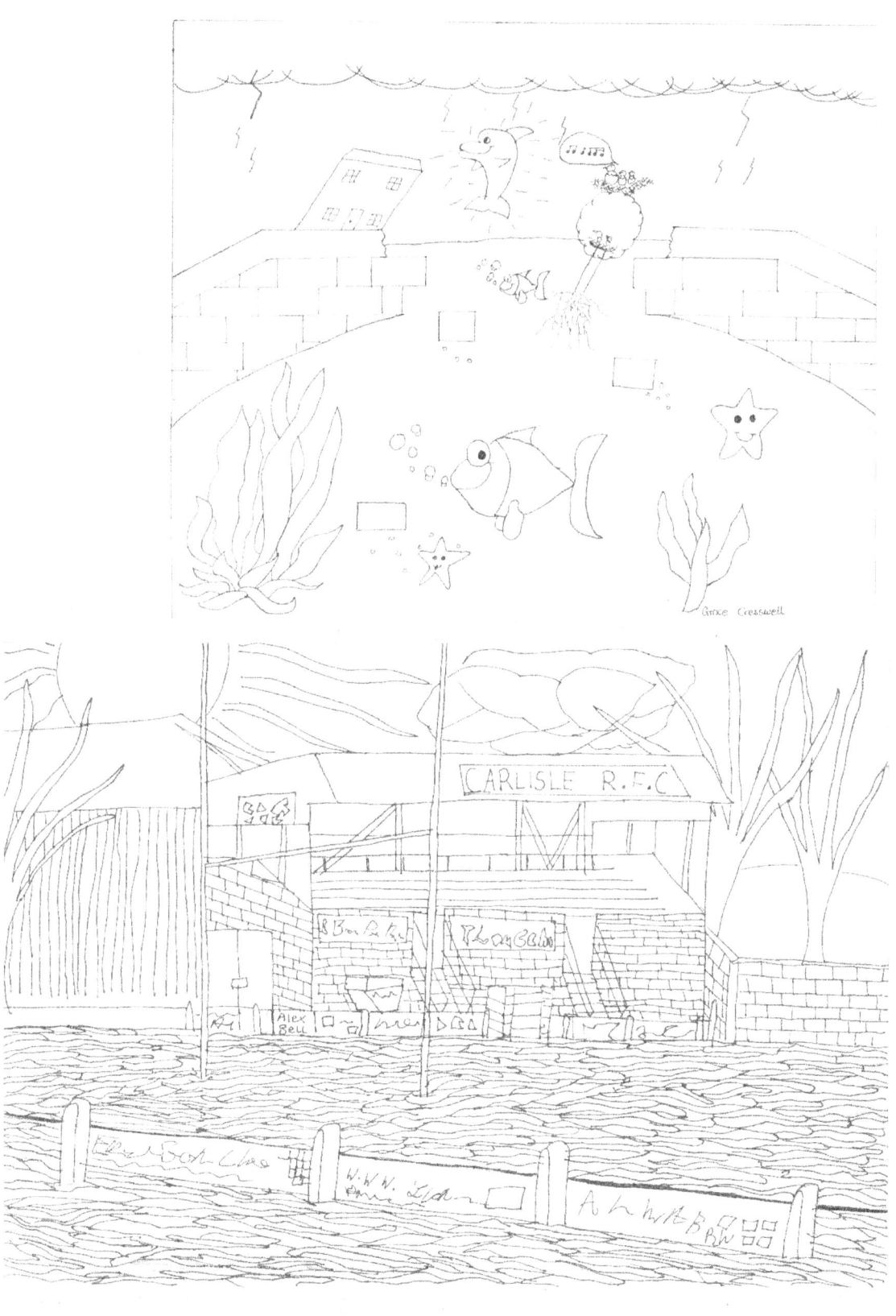

Grace Creswell QEGS

Alex Bell QEGS

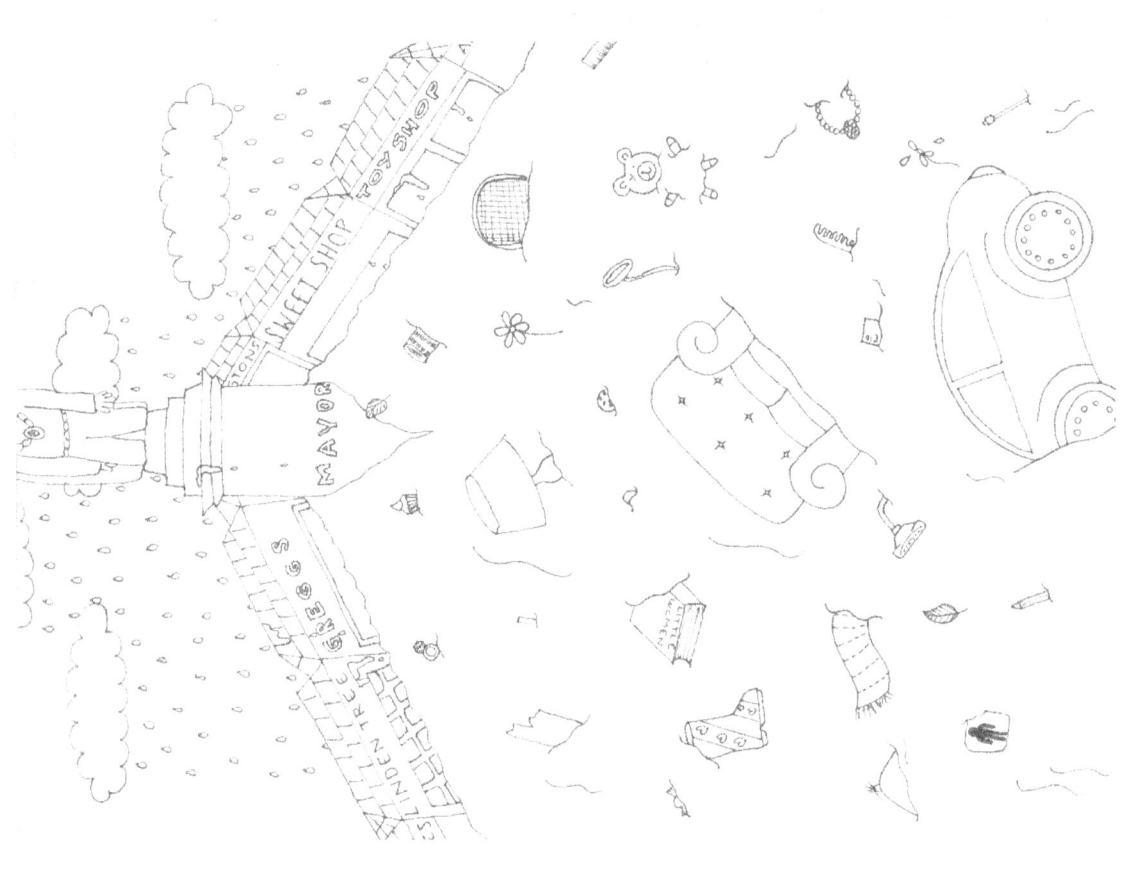

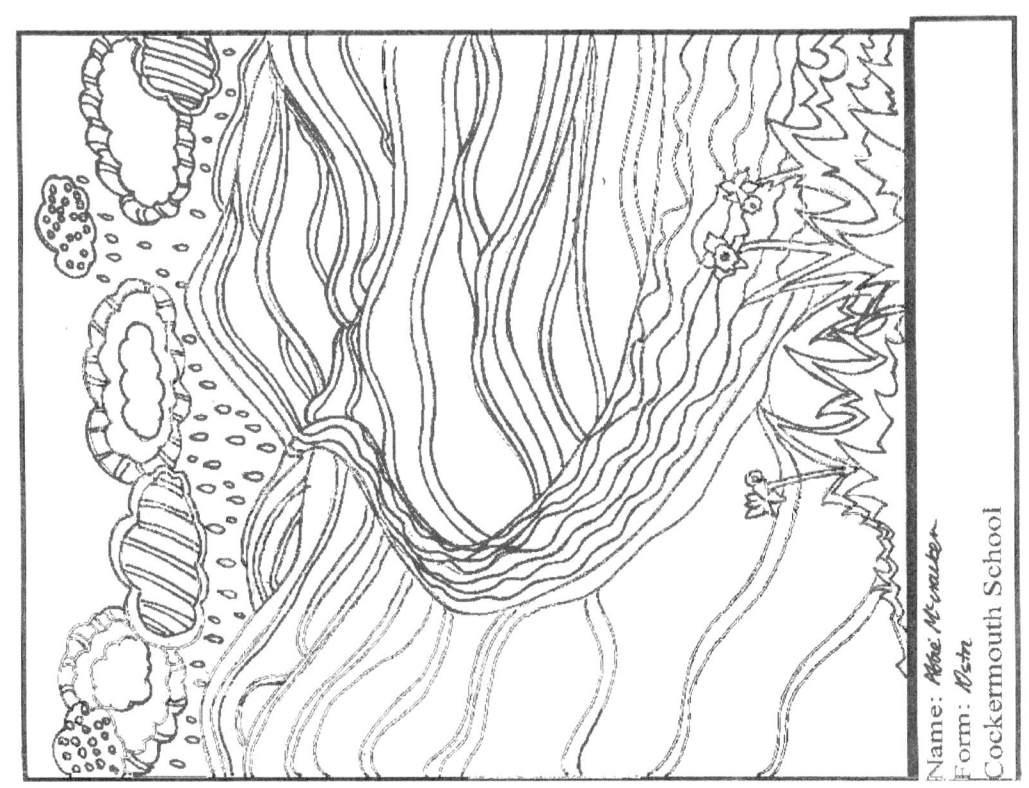

Name: *Abbe Minuten*
Form: *10th*
Cockermouth School

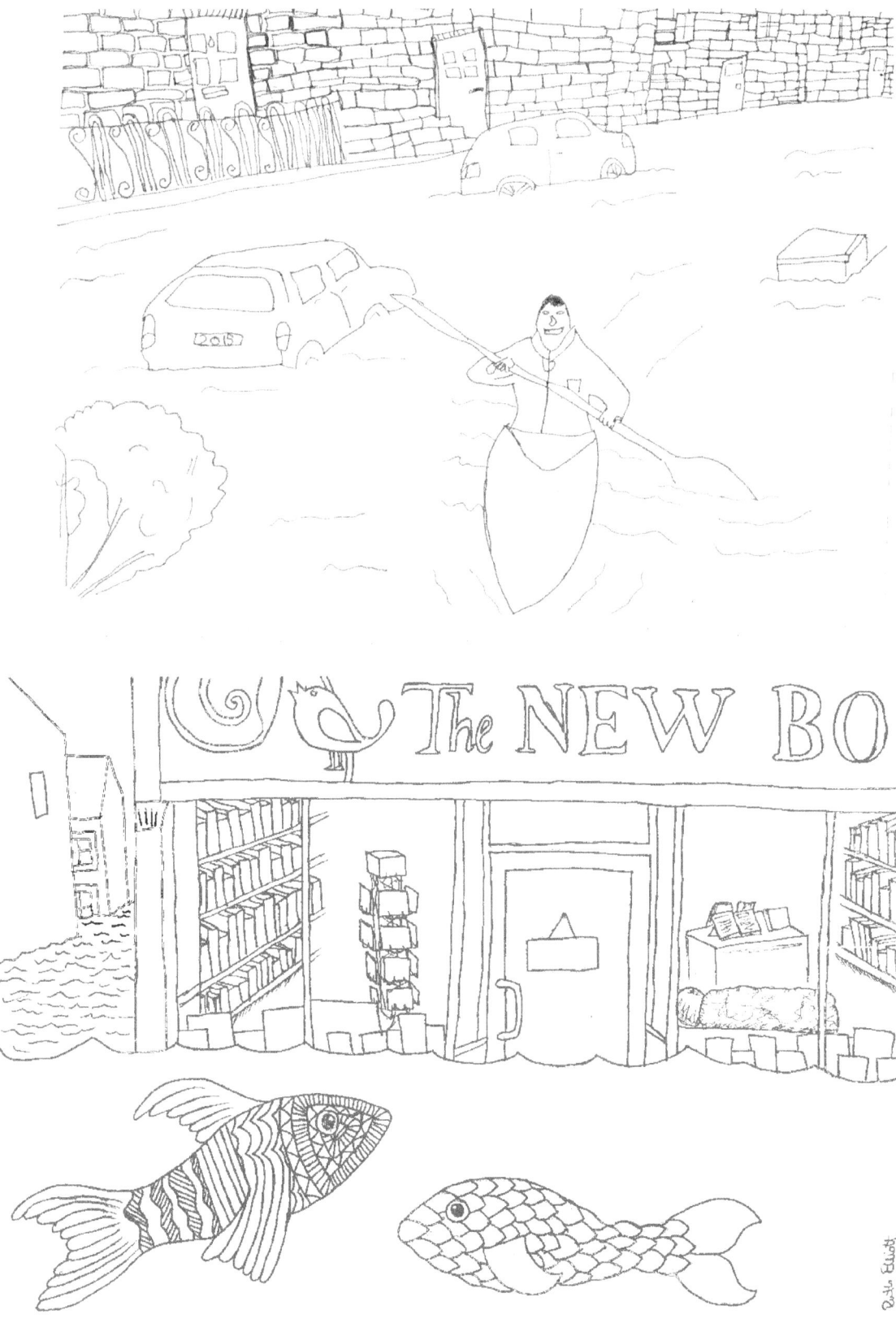

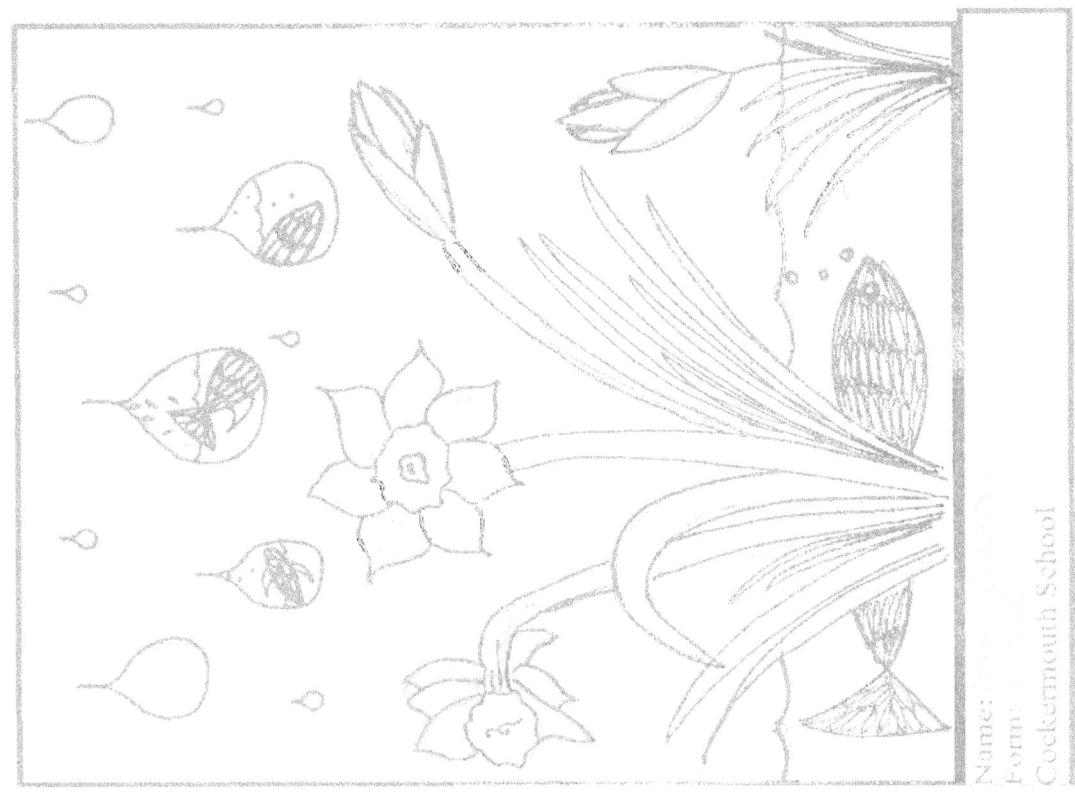

Name:
Form:
Cockermouth School

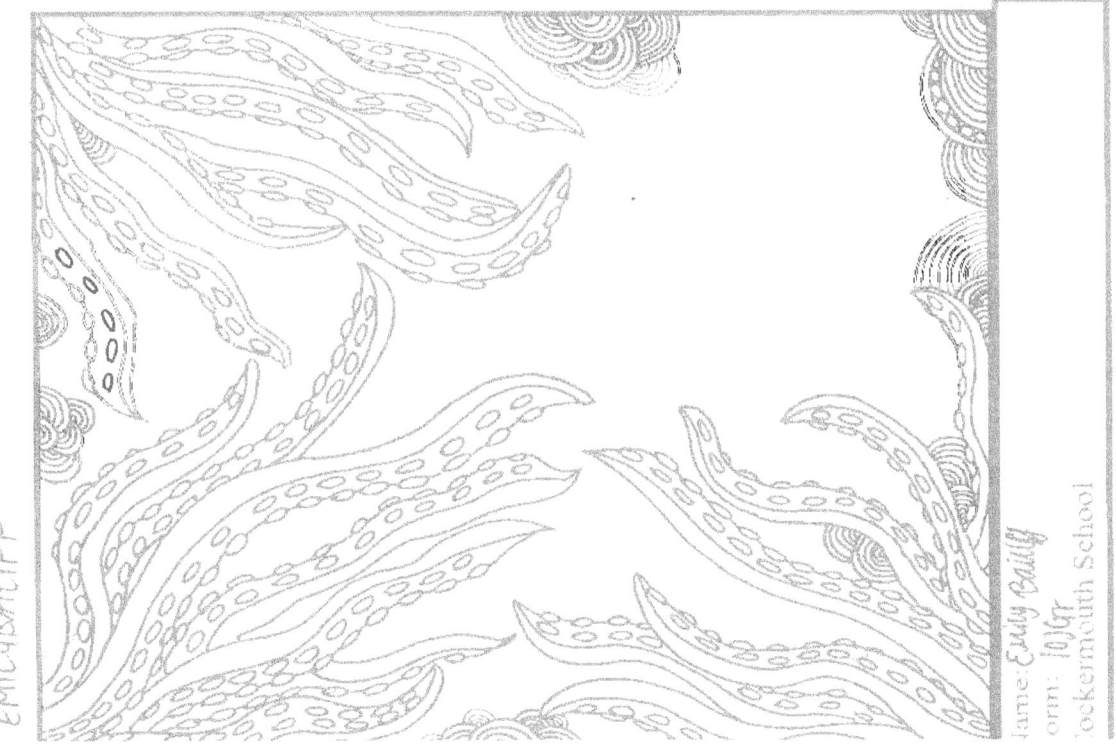

EMILY BAILIFF

Name: Emily Bailiff
Form: 10½r
Cockermouth School

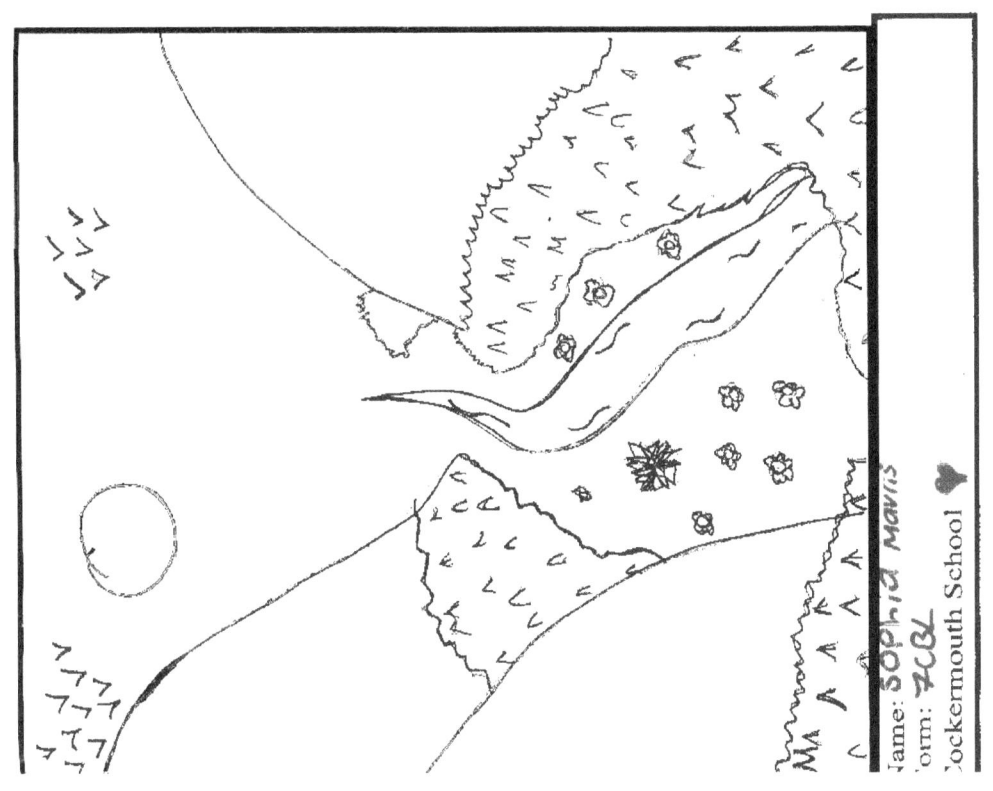

Name: Sophia Mavris
Form: 7CBL
Cockermouth School

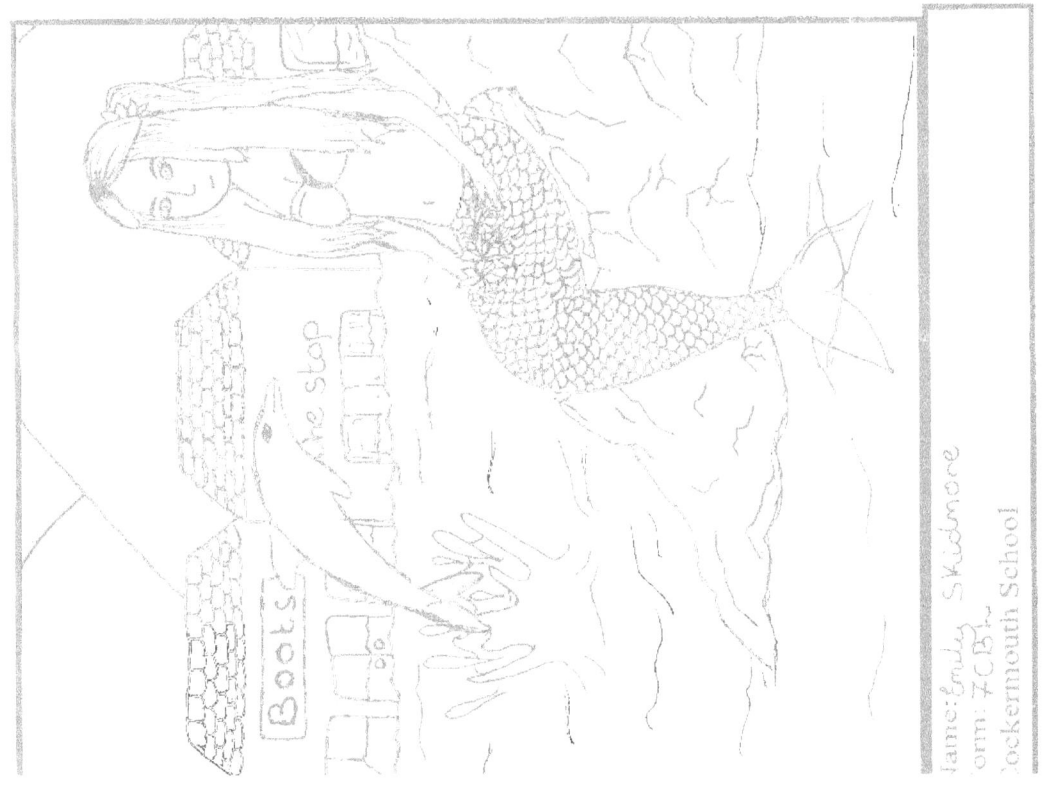

Name: Emily Skidmore
Form: 7CBL
Cockermouth School

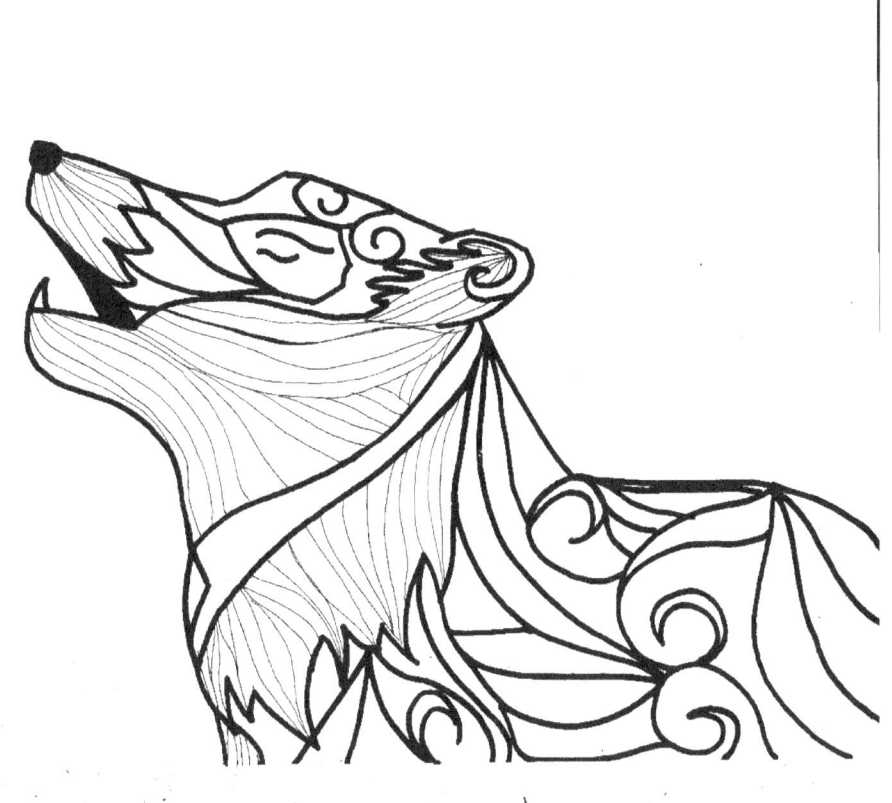

Mei Pollock

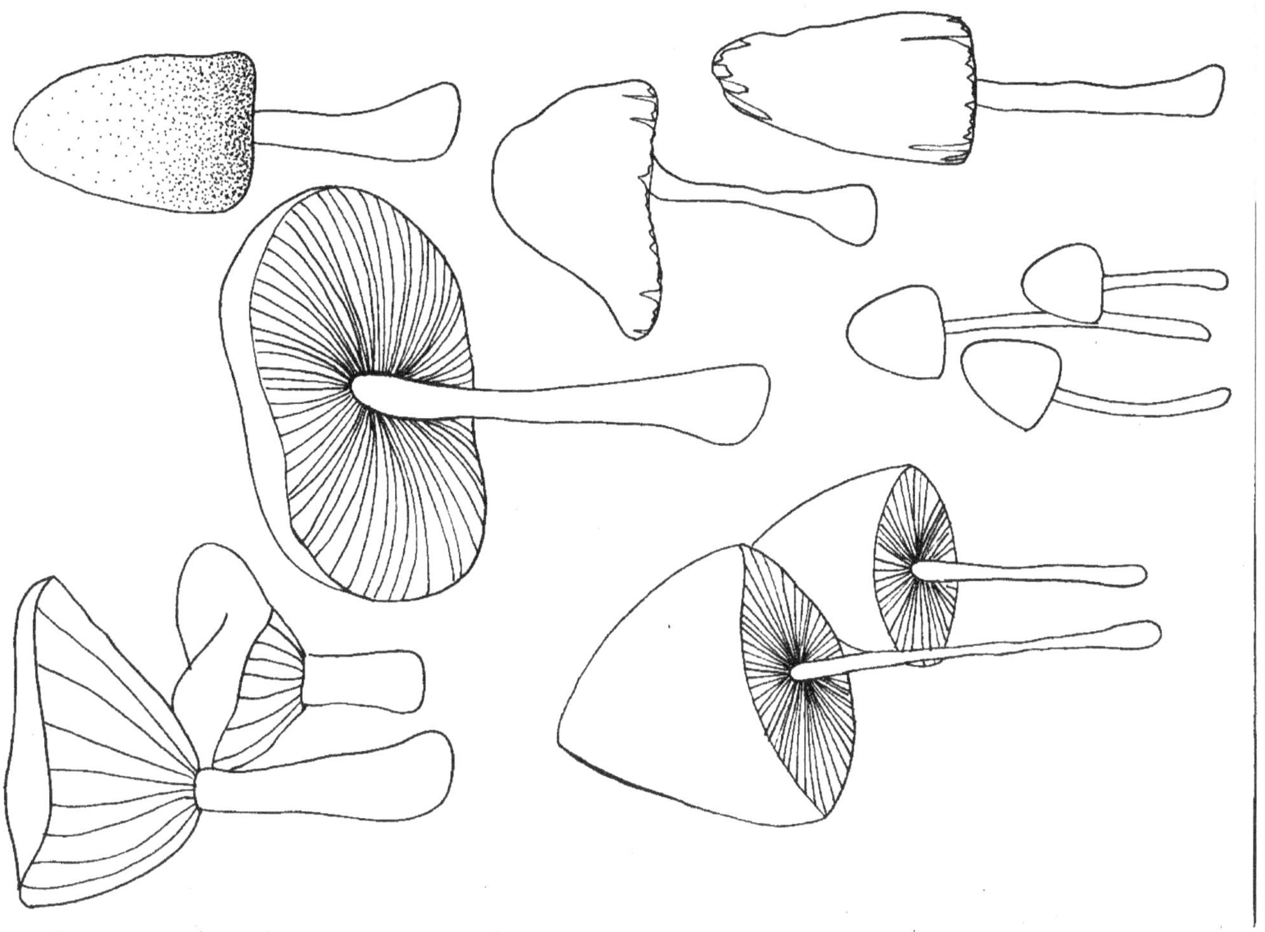

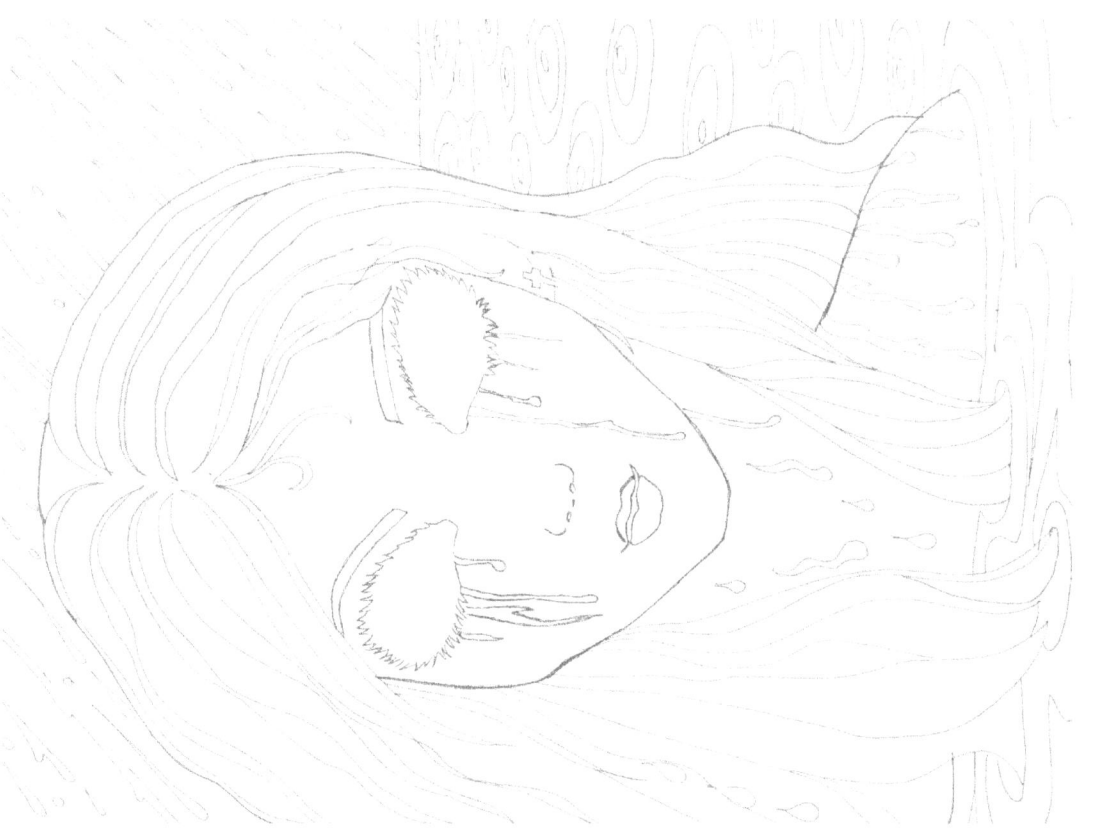

Asahi Pollock, Cockermouth School

Katie Jakob-Whitworth, Appleby School

Asahi Pollock, Cockermouth School

Katie Jakob-Whitworth, Appleby School